Cooking in High Cotton

Georgia Cotton Women

FATHER
&
SON
PUBLISHING, INC.
4909 N. Monroe Street • Tallahassee, Florida 32303
http://www.fatherson.com email: lance@fatherson.com
800-741-2712

Georgia Cotton Women, Inc.

P. O. Box 2186
Moultrie, GA 31776-2186
georgiacottonwomen@gmail.com
www.georgiacottonwomen.com

Georgia Cotton Women, Inc.
2009-10 Officers and Directors

President — Nancy Coleman, *Hartsfield*

Vice President — Charlotte Mathis, *Moultrie*

Chairman of Programs — Virginia Hart, *Moultrie*

Chairman of Membership — Charlotte Roberts, *Ocilla*

Chairman of Projects — Louise Milliron, *Shellman*

Secretary — Lynn Tillman, *Barney*

Treasurer — Shirley Tankersley, *Ocilla*

Past President — Beth Kirkland, *Nicholls*

Directors
Thelma Boykin, *Ocilla*
Cassandra Bullington, *Cordele*
Yvonne Crawford, *Chula*
Jane Gibbs, *Moultrie*
Cathy Thompson, *Pinehurst*
Mary Walker, *Tifton*
Charlotte Wingate, *Doerun*

HISTORY OF
GEORGIA COTTON WOMEN, INC.

In 1985, two wives of cotton farmers from the Mississippi Delta became alarmed at the lack of cotton clothes "Made in the USA" in their closets. They began a movement which evolved into the "Grown and Made in the USA, It Matters" campaign of the National Cotton Women's Committee of the National Cotton Council.

Julie Murphy from Brooks County, Georgia, attended a fashion show sponsored by this group at the Beltwide Cotton Conference and became interested in organizing a Cotton Women's group in Georgia. She solicited the help of Bardee Underwood of the National Cotton Council and at a meeting in Quitman in the fall of 1989, Georgia Cotton Wives was born. A year or so later the name was changed to Georgia Cotton Women to be more closely aligned with the national group. The group was later incorporated by the State of Georgia as a non-profit, educational group.

This group of volunteers spread the "Cotton" word throughout the state by organizing and presenting fashion shows, setting up exhibits at conventions, trade shows, state fairs, festivals, and the Sunbelt Agricultural Expo. The members participate in mall promotions, present programs to school children, distribute teaching kits to schools and extension groups across the state, and speak at civic groups. Members appear on radio and television. They even produced a television commercial promoting cotton and featuring members and their families. The group is headquartered in Moultrie, Georgia, in Colquitt County, one of the state's leading cotton-producing counties, but members come from all across the state, from cotton producing counties large and small.

The work of Georgia Cotton Women is financed with funds from the Georgia Cotton Commission which conducts programs of research, promotion, and education for Georgia's cotton producers. Funding for the Commission's programs comes from $1.00 per bale paid by Georgia's cotton producers. Through the benevolence of a producer/ginner, Georgia Cotton Women annually awards the Mobley scholarship to the son or daughter of a Georgia cotton producer. Through proceeds of this cookbook, a scholarship is presented annually to a child of anyone involved in the cotton industry, with priority given to children of members.

While the group encourages working to preserve agriculture in general and promotes a sense of camaraderie among its members, the main mission of the group is to promote the wonderful qualities of cotton and to educate our children and our communities that "Cotton Counts," it is a miracle of nature, and it IS "The Fabric of Our Lives."

ACKNOWLEDGMENTS

Georgia Cotton Women, Inc. gratefully acknowledges the contributions of all its members and friends who gave generously of their time and talents to make this cookbook possible.

Georgia Cotton Women also gratefully acknowledges the support of the Georgia Cotton Commission, whose generous financial support has made the organization's mission possible.

Georgia cotton facts and figures contained in this book were provided by the Commission and, unless otherwise stated, are based on 2006-07 statistics. Some information was gleaned from National Cotton Council and Cotton, Inc. publications.

Every effort has been made to ensure the accuracy of the recipes printed in this book.

ABOUT THIS BOOK

After years of tasting each other's good cooking at various functions, members of Georgia Cotton Women decided to publish a cookbook. But it wouldn't be just another cookbook. In addition to providing lots of good recipes with anecdotes from the cooks, the book would tell the story of the significance of cotton in Georgia. In 1997, the book was self-published and sold 2500 copies. Another 2500 copies were printed in 2000.

In 2008, the members decided to publish another book, this time utilizing the services of a cookbook publishing company to have a wider distribution. But the goal would be the same: to provide lots of good recipes with anecdotes from the cooks and to tell the story of cotton in Georgia. The result is this book.

Proceeds from the sale of this book will be used to fund scholarships to the children of GCW members or anyone involved in the cotton industry.

The print on the front cover was created by GCW member Cathy Thompson, an artist who enjoys capturing the beauty of cotton on paper and canvas. If you are interested in her work, contact her at 478-433-2905.

Table Of Contents

COOKING TIPS

Some recipes call for confectioners sugar while others call for powdered sugar. They are the same. In fact, the some companies label their product as "confectioners sugar;" some label it as "powdered sugar," while one uses "confectioners powdered sugar."

Basic equivalents:

3 teaspoons = 1 tablespoon   1 stick butter = ½ cup
4 tablespoons = ¼ cup   1 pound butter = 2 cups
8 tablespoons = ½ cup

When seeding jalapeño peppers, use rubber or plastic gloves and wash your hands immediately with soapy water when finished. The seeds and membranes are very hot and can burn your hands. Do not touch your eyes, nose or mouth before washing hands.

To make seeding jalapeño peppers easier, use a gadget made especially for that purpose. If you don't have one, use an apple corer. It's just the right size.

Many recipes call for a 1-pound box of powdered sugar. However, some stores only carry 2-pound bags. A 1-pound box of powdered sugar contains about 4 ½ cups, sifted.

When baking, don't use reduced fat or soft butter or margarine. They have a higher water content which diminishes the quality of baked goods.

Self-rising flour is all-purpose flour than has baking powder and salt added. Do NOT substitute self-rising for all-purpose. You can substitute all-purpose for self-rising by mixing 1 cup all-purpose flour with 1 teaspoon baking powder and ¼ teaspoon salt.

For a quick, disposable decorating bag , use a ziptop bag. Place the bag in a short glass and fold the top over the sides of the glass. Fill with frosting, whipped cream, melted chocolate, etc. Seal bag and snip off one corner of the bag and squeeze the contents out. The thickness of the contents will determine how large a hole you need. Whipped cream will require a larger hole than melted chocolate. No cleanup!!

Sprinkle apple or pear slices with lemon juice as soon as you slice them to prevent browning. If you're out of lemon juice, use a diet lemon-lime soft drink. It won't affect the taste of the fruit.

Appetizers and Beverages

THE PLANT

Perhaps one of the oldest fibers known to man, cotton is known to date back as far as 7,000 years. Natives of Egypt were making and wearing cotton clothing about 3,000 years before the birth of Christ. After all these years, cotton remains the most miraculous fiber under the sun.

The cotton plant is related to okra and hibiscus, both of which are also traditionally Southern plants. Cotton requires heat units to mature making it an ideal crop for Georgia and other Southern states.

The seeds are best planted the first ten days of May. The bloom, which is white when it opens and turns pink when it closes, lasts for only one day and first appears on the plant 60 days after it emerges from the soil. Bolls open 120 days after emergence with harvest at 150-160 days, usually in October and November.

While Sea Island cotton was the first cotton grown commercially in Georgia, it was the Upland variety that was to become the state's most valuable crop.

INDEX

Appetizers and Beverages

BEEF DIP
(A first edition favorite)

2	(8-ounce) packages cream cheese, softened
1	(4½ or 5 ounce) jar dried beef, chopped
½	cup sour cream or mayonnaise
2	tablespoons chopped onion (or more to taste)
2	tablespoons milk
1	teaspoon pepper

Beat cream cheese until smooth; add remaining ingredients and mix well. May be served hot or cold. To heat, place in 1-quart casserole and heat in 225 degree oven for 10 to 15 minutes. Serve with crackers. Yield: 1½ to 2 cups.

This dip is good enough to eat with a spoon.

Nancy Coleman
Hartsfield, Georgia

HAM DIP
(A first edition favorite)

1	(8-ounce) package cream cheese
1	(8-ounce) carton sour cream
1	(4 ½ or 5 ounce) jar dried beef, chopped OR
	Thin-sliced sandwich meat (ham, beef or turkey), chopped
2	tablespoons grated onion, optional

Mix in double boiler and heat. Serve warm or at room temperature. Reheat in microwave. Good with chips or crackers.

I'm continuously making this during the holidays.

Yvonne Crawford
Chula, Georgia

SUPER SPEEDY BLACK BEAN DIP

(A first edition favorite)

1   (11-ounce) can condensed black bean soup
1   cup shredded Cheddar cheese
½   cup picante sauce
½   teaspoon ground cumin
Dash of garlic powder

Mix all ingredients well in a small sauce pan. Heat, stirring frequently, until cheese is melted. Serve with chips, pita bread wedges or vegetables dippers.

My family enjoys this dip while watching football games. Go Dawgs!

Suellen Perry
Moultrie, Georgia

QUESO DIP

1   pound ground beef
1   (10-ounce) can diced tomatoes and green chilies
1   pound Velveeta cheese, cubed

Brown ground beef in skillet over medium heat; drain excess fat. Add tomatoes and chilies and cheese. Stir continuously until cheese is melted. Mixture will scorch easily. If serving over a long period of time, you may need to reheat or use a crock pot as it will thicken as it cools. Serve with corn chips or tortilla chips.

My son and his friends love this. Their name for it isn't very appetizing though – dog food!

Nancy Coleman
Hartsfield, Georgia

FABULOUS FRESH SALSA

1   clove garlic, minced
1   jalapeño pepper, seeded and minced
2   large fresh ripe tomatoes, diced
⅓   cup (loosely packed) chopped cilantro
1   medium Vidalia onion, finely chopped
1   tablespoon lime juice (fresh is better)
½   teaspoon salt
Coarse ground black pepper to taste

Mix all ingredients and serve with tortilla chips. You can adjust all ingredients to suit your taste. Best if tomatoes are ripe. Best when eaten within in a hour, but it can be refrigerated for a couple of hours. The mixture becomes bitter if kept overnight. Yield: about 2 cups

Once you've eaten fresh salsa made with homegrown tomatoes and peppers, you'll never want salsa from a jar again.

Nancy Coleman
Hartsfield, Georgia

GUACAMOLE PICA DE GALLO

2   medium ripe avocados (slight yield when mashed with thumb)
1   garlic, minced
2   tablespoons chopped cilantro
1   tablespoon lime juice (fresh is better)
1-2 jalapeño peppers, seeded and finely minced
¼   cup finely chopped onion
1   tomato, coarsely chopped
Salt and pepper to taste

Cut avocado in half, remove pit, and coarsely chop. Add remaining ingredients. Stir lightly so as not to mash the avocados. Ingredients may be adjusted to taste. Lay a piece of plastic wrap right on the surface of the guacamole so it doesn't brown and refrigerate until ready to serve.

I never liked guacamole until I had it prepared this way. Now my family and friends can't get enough of it.

Nancy Coleman
Hartsfield, Georgia

HOMEMADE SALSA

2	gallons of tomato chunks, peeled and cored, or chopped in blender
4	diced bell peppers
2	large diced onions
12	mild peppers or 2 habaneras, diced
¾	cup sugar
⅓	cup salt
1	cup white vinegar
1	(6-ounce) can tomato paste

Mix ingredients and cook on low heat approximately 45 minutes or until it is as thick as you want it. Yield: 8 quarts.

Mary Walker
Tifton, Georgia

LAYERED TACO DIP

(A first edition favorite)

1	can refried beans
1	(16-ounce) carton sour cream
1	(16-ounce) jar thick and chunky salsa
8	ounces Cheddar cheese, shredded
1	bunch green onions (use green tops only, snipped with scissors)
1	small can sliced black olives

Layer ingredients in the order listed above on a large round dish. Serve with Frito-Lay Scoops or Tostados Scoops.

Teenagers of all ages love this!!!

Charlotte Wingate
Doerun, Georgia

6

SAUSAGE LOVERS' DIP

1   (16-ounce) package mild pork sausage
2   tablespoons water
1   (10-ounce) package frozen chopped spinach, thawed,
    well drained
1   (8-ounce) package cream cheese, softened
1   (8-ounce) container sour cream
1   cup (4 ounces) shredded Cheddar cheese
1   (10-ounce) can diced tomatoes and green chilies, drained
½   cup chopped green onions
½   teaspoon garlic powder
Tortilla chips - or Toasted Pita Bread Triangles

Cook sausage in large skillet on medium high for about 10 minutes, stirring until
sausage crumbles and is no longer pink; drain. Stir in 2 tablespoons water, cover
and cook 1 minute. Stir in spinach, cream cheese, sour cream, shredded cheese,
tomatoes, onions, and garlic powder. Cook, stirring constantly, until thoroughly
heated. Serve with tortilla chips or pita triangles. Yield: about 4 cups.

The spinach gives this dip a little different flavor. Great for a party.

Charlotte Mathis
Moultrie, Georgia

HAM AND CHEESE BALL

1   (8-ounce) package cream cheese
¼   cup mayonnaise
1   (5-ounce) can chopped ham
1   tablespoon parsley flakes
1   teaspoon minced onion (optional)
¼   teaspoon dry mustard
¼   teaspoon hot pepper sauce
½   cup chopped nuts (your choice)

Beat cream cheese and mayonnaise. Add next 5 ingredients. Chill in refrigerator.
Form into ball and roll in nuts.

I make several of these during Christmas. They are good for receptions also.
May be frozen and used later if left over.

Yvonne Crawford
Chula, Georgia

SPINACH DIP IN THE "ROUND"

(A first edition favorite)

1   (10-ounce) package frozen chopped spinach, thawed, drained and squeezed
1   (2¼-ounce) package dried vegetable soup mix
1   (8-ounce) can water chestnuts, chopped
6   green onions, chopped (tops and bottoms)
1   cup mayonnaise
1½ cups sour cream
1   loaf round bread

Mix all ingredients together except bread. Chill overnight to combine flavors. Just before serving, scoop out large area in center of bread, cutting scooped out bread into small squares. Spoon dip into center and arrange bread cubes around bread ring. For extra cubes of bread, cut a loaf of French bread into cubes. Yield: 25 servings

I kept score for Tiftarea Academy's basketball team for a number of years. The first time I tasted this recipe was at Crisp Academy in Cordele during state playoffs one spring. It was and is still WONDERFUL!!

Mary Register
Waterloo, Georgia

SPINACH DIP

2   cups mayonnaise
2   cups sour cream
1   (16-ounce) package frozen chopped spinach (cooked in microwave and squeezed dry)
1   can artichokes, chopped
2   cups grated Parmesan cheese
8   ounces shredded Parmesan cheese
Seasoned salt and pepper to taste
8   ounces shredded Mozzarella cheese

Mix all ingredients in order listed. Top with Mozzarella cheese and bake at 350 degrees for 20- 25 minutes or until bubbly. Serve with toast points or Frito Scoops.

Andy Gibbs
Atlanta, Georgia

Appetizers and Beverages

SPINACH DIPPING SAUCE

1   (4-ounce) can green chilies, finely chopped
1   medium onion, chopped
2   tablespoons vegetable oil
2   tomatoes, peeled, seeded and chopped
1   (10-ounce) package frozen chopped spinach, thawed and
     squeezed dry
1½   tablespoons red wine vinegar
1   (8-ounce) package cream cheese, softened
1   (8-ounce) package Monterey Jack cheese, grated
1   cup half-and-half
Salt, pepper and paprika to taste

In a small skillet, sauté chilies and onion in oil for 4 minutes or until soft.
Add chopped tomatoes and cook, stirring constantly, for 5 minutes. Remove
from heat and transfer to mixing bowl. Stir in spinach, vinegar, cream cheese,
Monterey Jack cheese, half and half, salt and pepper. Pour mixture into a greased
baking dish. Sprinkle with paprika. Bake at 400 degrees for 20 to 25 minutes.
Serve with scoops. Yield: 4 cups

Virginia Hart
Moultrie, Georgia

VIDALIA ONION DIP

2   cups finely chopped Vidalia onions
2   cups mayonnaise
2   cups grated extra-sharp Cheddar cheese
Tabasco sauce to taste (optional)

Mix all ingredients together and bake in a 2-quart casserole dish at 350 degrees
for 30 minutes or until bubbly. Serve with Triscuits or crackers of your choice.

*Pam Rojas gave me this recipe when our boys were playing baseball together
in middle school. They have both since graduated and this is still a favorite
recipe.*

Nancy Coleman
Hartsfield, Georgia

BAKED ONION DIP

2   cups chopped Vidalia onions
1   cup Hellman's mayonnaise
1   cup Parmesan cheese, shredded, not grated, if possible
1   cup shredded Swiss cheese
Pepper to taste

Mix together. Put the mixture in a sprayed 9x13-inch casserole dish and bake until bubbly and browned on top. Best if refrigerated overnight before baking. Serve with saltine crackers.

Virginia Hart
Moultrie, Georgia

CHARLESTON CHEESE DIP

1   (8-ounce) package cream cheese
1   green onion, chopped
1   cup mayonnaise or Miracle Whip
1   (28-ounce) package bacon bits
½   cup grated cheese
5-6 crumbed Ritz crackers

Mix cream cheese, onions, mayonnaise, bacon bits, cheese and crackers; place in baking dish. Crumble extra crackers and add more cheese on top. Bake at 375 degrees for 15-20 minutes; then top with bacon. Serve with crackers or corn chips.

Tonya Loraine Bustle
Coolidge, Georgia

CHEESE BALL

(A first edition favorite)

2   (8-ounce) packages cream cheese
1   (8-ounce) package Cheddar cheese, grated
1   tablespoon chopped green pepper
1   tablespoon chopped pimento
2   teaspoons Worcestershire sauce
Dash cayenne pepper and salt
Pecans, finely chopped

Mix all ingredients together until well blended. Shape into ball. Roll in pecans. Wrap in plastic wrap. Chill 24 hours. Makes 2 balls.

This is my favorite and is so good.

Gail Thompson
Moultrie, Georgia

ROSALYN CARTER'S CHEESE RING

1   pound (4 cups) sharp Cheddar cheese, grated
1   cup mayonnaise
3   ounces cream cheese
1   cup chopped pecans
1   small onion, chopped
Dash cayenne pepper
Dash white pepper

Mix all ingredients together and place in ring mold. Chill over night. When ready to serve, invert on serving plate. Make a small indention in mold and fill with strawberry preserves or pepper jelly. Serve with bagel chips, Triscuits or Wheat Thins.

I got this recipe from my brother who worked at Georgia Southwestern State University where President and Mrs. Carter were actively involved in campus affairs. It was a recipe the food service staff prepared at her request. It's better not to place the jelly directly on the cheese ring, but in a small bowl. It's easier to store leftovers if there isn't jelly on the cheese ring.

Nancy Coleman,
Hartsfield, Georgia

CREAM CHEESE SPREAD

2   (8-ounce) packages cream cheese
1   cup whipping cream, unwhipped
½   teaspoon salt
1 ½   teaspoon herb seasoning
½   teaspoon dried crushed red pepper
½   cup chopped roasted pecans
Sweet onion pepper jelly

In a medium mixing bowl, beat cream cheese until soft. Add 2 tablespoons whipping cream, salt and seasonings to taste. In small bowl, beat remaining whipped cream until holds soft peaks. Fold whipped cream and pecans into cream cheese mixture. Pour in to mold and chill. When ready to serve, remove from mold and top with sweet onion pepper jelly. Serve with crackers.

This was used at my retirement tea and was a hit! It's unusual but very good.

Jane Gibbs
Moultrie, Georgia

CRANBERRY CHEESE BALL

2   (8-ounce) packages cream cheese
1   (8-ounce) can crushed pineapple, drained
2   cups chopped pecans
2   tablespoons green onions, chopped
1   teaspoon salt
1   large bag Craisins

In bowl, beat cream cheese until smooth and creamy. Gradually stir in pineapple, pecans, onion, and Craisins. Refrigerate until firm. Form into pineapple shape; use whole pecans and fresh pineapple top to garnish.

Gail Thompson
Moultrie, Georgia

Appetizers and Beverages

PARTY SANDWICH FILLING

8   ounces cream cheese
¼   cup chopped green peppers
3   tablespoons chopped pimiento
¾   teaspoon salt
3   hard-cooked eggs, chopped
¾   cup chopped nuts
¼   cup chopped onion
1   tablespoon catsup
Dash of lemon pepper

Mix together and spread on sandwich bread.

Brenda Morris
Ocilla, Georgia

SHIRLEY'S PIMIENTO CHEESE

8   ounces mild Cheddar cheese
8   ounces sharp or medium Cheddar cheese
4   ounces diced pimientos
2   tablespoons Splenda
1 ½ cups Blue Plate mayonnaise

Grate cheese. Add pimientos with juice (do not drain) to cheese. Add Splenda and mayonnaise. Mix well.

A recipe given to me by Shirley Mims, long-time Colquitt County school nutrition manager.

Virginia Hart
Moultrie, Georgia

FRUIT DIP

2   (8-ounce) packages cream cheese, softened
2   (7-ounce) jars marshmallow crème
3   tablespoons brown sugar
1   (12-ounce) container whipped topping, thawed
1   teaspoon vanilla extract

Cream together the cream cheese, marshmallow crème, and brown sugar. Beat until smooth. When well blended, fold in whipped topping and vanilla. Refrigerate until serving. Serve with fresh fruit.

Virginia Hart
Moultrie, Georgia

CHEESE PUFFS

1   (16-ounce) loaf French bread
½   cup butter or margarine
1   cup (4 ounces) shredded sharp Cheddar cheese
1   (3-ounce) package cream cheese
2   egg whites

Trim crust from bread; discard crusts. Cut bread into 2-inch cubes; place in large bowl. Melt butter, Cheddar cheese and cream cheese in saucepan over low heat; stir occasionally. Beat whites at high speed with an electric mixer until stiff peaks form; fold one-quarter of egg whites into cheese mixture. Fold cheese mixture into remaining egg whites. Pour over bread cubes, tossing to coat. Place bread cubes in single layer on an ungreased cookie sheet. Bake at 400 degrees for 12 minutes or until golden.

Jane Gibbs
Moultrie, Georgia

Appetizers and Beverages

CHEESE WAFERS

3   cups crisp rice cereal
1   (8-ounce) package extra sharp Cheddar cheese
2   cups all-purpose flour
1   cup (2 sticks) margarine, softened
1   teaspoon Tabasco sauce (or more to taste)
½   teaspoon salt

Grate cheese and mix all ingredients together until butter becomes soft. Make a big ball; pinch off small pieces and roll into balls. Place on lightly greased cooking sheet and press down lightly with fingers. (You can flatten with fork). Bake at 350 degrees for 8-10 minutes (will not be brown). For crispier wafers, bake 15-20 minutes at 375 degrees. Yield: 7 dozen.

Don't use packaged grated cheese – it won't blend as well as freshly grated cheese.

Nancy Coleman
Hartsfield, Georgia

CHEESE STRAWS WITH PECANS

1   pound sharp cheese, grated
1   cup all-purpose flour
1   cup pecans, chopped
1½   sticks butter or margarine
½   teaspoon salt
½   teaspoon red pepper

Knead grated cheese with butter and flour, salt and pepper. Add chopped nuts and make into a roll. Refrigerate overnight. Slice as thin as possible and bake on ungreased cookie sheet at 400 degrees for about 10 minutes. Remove when golden and crisp. Yield: 4 dozen.

These are so easy and are great for parties.

Charlotte Mathis
Moultrie, Georgia

Appetizers and Beverages

BOILED GEORGIA PEANUTS

(A first edition favorite)

1   gallon fresh-picked green peanuts
1   cup salt

Place peanuts in large pot and cover with water. Bring to a boil and add salt. Boil for 1 hour. Pour off salted water and rinse well with cold water.

Eat and enjoy!!!

Kenneth Thompson
Pinehurst, Georgia

ROASTED PECAN HALVES

(A first edition favorite)

4   cups pecan halves
¼   cup (½ stick) margarine
Salt

Place pecan halves on a microwave baking dish. Spread evenly in single layer. Cook at high temperature for 5 minutes. Mix butter with the nuts while hot. Place back on baking dish and sprinkle with salt. Return to microwave and cook on high temperature for 2 additional minutes. You will have more than one cooking. Cooking time will vary according to the amount of nuts on your dish.

These nuts are delicious to serve at any receptions. If any of my friends have a wedding or reception in their family, they always ask me to roast the nuts. It's a very easy dish to prepare.

Ilene Coleman
Moultrie, Georgia

WHITE TRASH PARTY SNACK

3	cups Rice Chex
3	cups Corn Chex
3	cups Cherrios
2	cups small pretzels
2	cups roasted pecan halves
12	ounce package plain M & M's
1½	pounds vanilla almond bark

Mix all ingredients except almond bark in large bowl. Melt almond bark. Pour over mixture and mix well. Spread on waxed paper. Let cool and break into pieces.

Bag in cellophane bags for gift-giving.

Louise Milliron,
Shellman, Georgia

OLIVE BITES
(A first edition favorite)

½	pound sharp Cheddar cheese, grated
¼	cup butter
1	cup sifted all-purpose flour
½	teaspoon garlic salt
¼	teaspoon salt
	Dash cayenne pepper
1	(10-ounce) jar small pimento stuffed olives

Bring cheese and butter to room temperature. Sift together flour, garlic salt, salt and cayenne pepper. Preheat oven to 350 degrees. Cream cheese and butter together in large bowl of electric mixer; add flour mixture. Mix well with spoon or hand. Use hands to form mixture into a ball. Knead several times. Drain olives and dry on paper towel. Shape pieces of dough around olives with thin layer of dough. Place on ungreased baking sheet and bake for 25 minutes or until light golden. If desired, olive bites may be made ahead of time and placed on a cookie sheet, then placed in freezer. When they are thoroughly frozen, transfer to plastic bag or freezer container and keep until needed. May be baked frozen in a preheated 350 degree oven for 25 minutes or until light golden. Yield: approximately 6 dozen.

Serve hot!! Enjoy!

Connie Mobley
Moultrie, Georgia

OYSTER CRACKERS

¾   cup salad oil
1   package (1 ounce) buttermilk recipe original ranch salad
    dressing mix
½   teaspoon dill weed
¼   teaspoon lemon pepper
¼   teaspoon garlic powder
1   (12-16 ounce) bag plain oyster crackers (I use miniature)

Whisk together oil, salad dressing mix, dill weed, lemon pepper, and garlic powder. Pour over crackers, stirring to coat. Place on baking sheet and bake at 275 degrees for 15 minutes. Cool and store in airtight container. Makes 11-12 cups.

Brenda Morris
Ocilla, Georgia

TROPICAL SNACK MIX

12   cups popped popcorn
1   cup chopped macadamia nuts
1   (7-ounce) package tropical blend mixed dried fruit bits
½   cup dried cranberries
½   cup butter
1   cup granulated sugar
1   teaspoon finely shredded lime peel
1   teaspoon finely shredded orange peel
½   teaspoon ground ginger

Preheat oven to 300 degrees. Remove all unpopped kernels from popped popcorn. In a large roasting pan combine the popcorn, nuts, fruit bits, and cranberries and set aside. In a small saucepan combine butter, sugar, lime peel, orange peel and ginger. Cook and stir over medium heat until butter is melted and mixture is nearly smooth. The sugar will not completely dissolve. Pour mixture over popcorn mixture and stir gently to coat. Bake 45 minutes, stirring every 15 minutes. Remove from oven and spread mixture on a large piece of foil to cool. Store in an airtight container up to 1 week. Yield: about fifteen 1 cup servings.

Margaret Anderson
Meigs, Georgia

Appetizers and Beverages

VEGGIE CHEESE BARS

2   (8-ounce) packages crescent dinner rolls
2   (8-ounce) packages cream cheese, softened
¼   cup mayonnaise (regular works better than light)
1   envelope ranch dressing mix
Broccoli, finely chopped
Green and red peppers, finely chopped
Tomatoes, finely chopped
¾   cup mild Cheddar cheese, grated

Unroll crescent rolls. Place on greased cookie sheet; press edges together to make one large sheet of dough. Bake 350 degrees for 7-10 minutes until lightly browned. Cool completely. Combine cream cheese, mayonnaise and ranch dressing mix. Beat until smooth. Spread on cooled rolls. Sprinkle chopped vegetables on top. Sprinkle grated cheese on top of vegetables. Refrigerate until ready to serve. Cut into small squares.

Nancy Coleman
Hartsfield, Georgia

BACON ROLL-UPS

¼   cup butter or margarine
½   cup water
1 ½ cups packaged herb-seasoned stuffing
1   egg, slightly beaten
¼   pound hot bulk pork sausage
½ to ⅔ pound sliced bacon

Melt butter in water in saucepan. Remove from heat; stir into stuffing, then add egg and sausage. Blend thoroughly. Chill for about an hour for easier handling, then shape into small oblongs about the size of pecans. Cut bacon strips into thirds, crosswise; wrap one piece around dressing mixture and fasten with wooden pick. Place on rack in shallow pan and bake at 375 degrees for 35 minutes, or until brown and crisp, turning at halfway point in cooking. Drain on paper towels and serve hot. May be made the day before baking; also freezes well before baking. Yield: about 36 appetizers.

Angela Gibbs White
Pearson, Georgia

Appetizers and Beverages

SAUSAGE BALLS

3   cups biscuit mix
1   pound sharp Cheddar cheese, grated
1   pound bulk sausage

Mix ingredients until thoroughly mixed. This has to be done by hand as mixture is very stiff. Pinch off and roll into small balls. Bake at 350 degrees 15 to 20 minutes.

Variation: Use hot sausage and 8 ounces of pepper jack cheese and 8 ounces of Colby cheese.

If you want it a little hotter, after mixing together well, add 1 tablespoon (or more if your desire) of hot sauce and mix again. It's best to grate the cheese yourself rather than buying packaged grated cheese. Freshly grated cheese mixes better.

Nancy Coleman
Hartsfield, Georgia

PIZZA ROUNDS

1   pound ground beef
1   pound sausage, mild or hot (I use mild)
1   pound Velveeta cheese, cut into cubes
1   package wheat sub rolls, cut in thin slices

Brown ground beef and sausage in skillet; drain well. Add cheese to skillet and stir until it melts. Spread mixture on bread slices. Sprinkle with garlic salt or seasoning of your choice. Broil in oven until crispy. You can make ahead of time and freeze and use as you want. Bake them at 350 degrees when they are frozen.

Kathy Wright bakes these at the church choir party she hosts each year at Christmas. We eat them faster than she can make them.

Nancy Coleman
Hartsfield, Georgia

Appetizers and Beverages

BARBECUED SAUSAGE BALLS

(A first edition favorite)

1	pound hot or mild bulk pork sausage
1/3	cup seasoned bread crumbs or dry herb stuffing
1	egg, slightly beaten
1/4	teaspoon ground sage
1/4	cup chili sauce
2	tablespoons brown sugar
1/2	cup water
1/4	cup catsup
1	tablespoon soy sauce
1	tablespoon vinegar

Combine sausage, bread crumbs, egg, and sage; mix thoroughly. Shape into balls the size of a pecan. Brown on all sides in dry skillet; drain on paper towels. Drain fat from skillet and then add catsup, chili sauce, soy sauce, brown sugar, vinegar, and 1/2 cup water; stir well. Return meatballs to skillet, cover and simmer for 30 minutes. Refrigerate or freeze. When ready to serve, reheat, place in chafing dish and serve with cocktail picks. Yield: Approximately 3 to 5 dozen, depending on size. Triple the recipe for a cocktail supper for about 50 people.

Somewhat time-consuming and messy to prepare, but the raves will be worth the effort. A good make-ahead recipe. I always double the recipe and never have any left over.

Nancy Coleman
Hartsfield, Georgia

MINIATURE SAUSAGE MUFFINS

½   pound mild bulk pork sausage
⅓   cup chopped onions
1   (6-ounce) package biscuit mix
¼   teaspoon ground pepper
½   teaspoon mustard
½   cup milk
½   cup (2 ounces) finely shredded Cheddar cheese

Combine sausage and onion in skillet. Cover over medium heat until browned, stirring to crumble. Drain well. Combine biscuit mix, mustard, pepper; add milk, stirring just until moistened. Stir in sausage mixture and cheese (mixture will be thick). Spoon into greased muffin pans, filling ⅔ full. Bake at 400 degrees for 12-14 minutes or until golden brown. Remove from pans immediately.

Charlotte Mathis
Moultrie, Georgia

KELLY'S SOUTH GEORGIA CAVIAR

2   (15 ounce) cans black-eyed peas, drained
1   (15 ounce) cans yellow whole kernel corn, drained
1   (15 ounce) can white corn, drained
1   (15 ounce) can petite stewed tomatoes
1   small onion, chopped
Sliced jalapeño peppers, to your taste
2   tablespoons Italian dressing

Mix all ingredients together and serve with scoop Fritos.

Kelly Thompson McCabe
Thomasville, Georgia

ILENE'S PUNCH

1   (46-ounce) can pineapple juice
3   (6-ounce) cans lemonade concentrate, undiluted
1   cup sugar
1   (2-liter) bottle ginger ale

Mix pineapple juice, sugar, and lemonade concentrate in gallon jug. Add water to fill jug. Freeze. About 12 hours prior to serving, remove from freezer for slush consistency. (If you use a milk jug, you will probably need to cut the neck off to remove mixture from jug.) Mix punch slush with ginger ale in punch bowl just prior to serving. Can be made without freezing. Can be tinted pink or green with food coloring. Yield: About 35 5-ounce servings.

A Coleman family recipe. Used at all family weddings, showers, and parties.

Ilene Coleman
Moultrie, Georgia

PERKED PUNCH

6   cups cranberry juice
8   cups apple juice
1/3 cup brown sugar
1/2 teaspoon salt
1/2 teaspoon whole cloves
4   cinnamon sticks

Put juices in percolator; put dry ingredients in basket; perk. Remove basket when perked.

* May use Aspen Mix:
    1/2 cup mix
    2   cinnamon sticks
    1/4 teaspoon cloves
    Salt

Yvonne Crawford
Chula, Georgia

WARM CHRISTMAS PUNCH

1   gallon apple juice
1   (7-ounce) package Red Hot cinnamon candies

In a 3-quart slow cooker, combine juice and Red Hots. Cook on low for 2-5 hours. You may also put the Red Hots in basket of a 32-cup percolator and the juice in the bottom; perk until Red Hots melt. If you don't have a slow-cooker or percolator, just put the juice and Red Hots in large pot on the stove and simmer until Red Hots are melted.

Delicious and makes the house smells like Christmas.

Nancy Coleman
Hartsfield, Georgia

CRANBERRY SPARKLE

1   (12-ounce) can frozen cranberry juice concentrate, thawed
      and undiluted
1   (2-liter) bottle ginger ale, chilled

Mix gently in punch bowl or large pitcher. Serve immediately. Can be served over crushed ice. Yield: about 13 (5 ounce) servings. Variation: Substitute 12 ounces of lemonade concentrate

A delicious, tart, and bubbly, non-alcoholic beverage.

Nancy Coleman
Hartsfield, Georgia

MOCHA ICE CREAM PUNCH

6   cups chilled milk
1   cup chocolate syrup
Pinch salt
3   pint vanilla ice cream
6   tablespoons instant coffee
½   cup hot water

Dissolve instant coffee in hot water; add to chocolate syrup. Blend with milk in punch bowl. Stir in softened ice cream. Serve immediately. Yield: 15 to 20 servings.

An excellent choice for a morning shower or reception. A wonderful flavor and I don't even like coffee.

Nancy Coleman
Hartsfield, Georgia

EASY PUNCH

2   large cans of pineapple juice
2   (2-liter) bottles of citrus/grapefruit soda (Fresca, Freshie, or Wink)
1   (12-ounce) can frozen lemonade concentrate
1   (2-liter) bottle 7-Up

Mix and chill. Yield: 50 servings

Gail Thompson
Moultrie, Georgia

KOOL-AID PUNCH

2	packages cherry Kool-Aid
1	package orange Kool-Aid
1	(46-ounce) can pineapple juice
1	teaspoon almond flavoring
1	(2-liter) bottle ginger ale

Mix Kool-Aid as directed on packages. Add pineapple juice and almond flavoring. Chill until ready to serve. Add ginger ale at the last minute. Yield: 2 gallons

Gail Thompson
Moultrie, Georgia

Appetizers and Beverages

Breads

THE EARLY YEARS

Cotton was first planted in Georgia near Savannah in 1734, just one year after the state was settled, using seed brought from England. Prior to discovering the potential of producing cotton commercially in Georgia, the state's main crops were silk, rice and indigo.

In the early years, Georgia was noted for its production of the famous extra-long staple Sea Island cotton. While Sea Island cotton was an extremely valuable commodity, it could only be grown on the coast. It was the short-staple Upland cotton that produced the great revolution in Georgia agriculture. Though cotton was grown in other colonies, Georgia was the largest producer.

One farm hand could work four acres of cotton, all cultivation done with a hoe. Production was roughly 350 pounds per acre. To separate one pound of lint from the seed required one day's work, usually done at night during the winter months around the fire.

For over 100 years, from the time cotton was first planted in Georgia in 1733, until the beginning of the Civil War in 1861, cotton was the most successfully grown commercial crop in the state.

INDEX

BUTTERMILK BISCUITS

2 ½ cups self-rising flour
1½ teaspoons baking powder
1½ teaspoons sugar
⅓ cup shortening
1 cup buttermilk
Melted butter

Combine flour, baking powder, and sugar; mix well. Cut in shortening with a pastry blender until mixture resembles coarse meal. Add buttermilk, stirring until dry ingredients are moistened. Turn dough out onto a lightly floured surface; knead lightly 3 or 4 times. Roll out and cut. Bake at 375 degrees for 18 minutes. Brush tops with melted butter.

Sheila Brown
Moultrie, Georgia

CHEESE BISCUITS

2 cups self-rising flour
1½ sticks margarine, softened
2 cups grated sharp Cheddar cheese
8 ounces sour cream

Mix all together. Bake in muffin pans greased with cooking spray at 400 degrees for 12 -15 minutes.

Margaret Anderson
Meigs, Georgia

HERB ROLLS
(A first edition favorite)

¼   cup margarine
1 ½ teaspoon parsley flakes
½   teaspoon dill weed
½   teaspoon bottled minced onion
1   package (10-count) buttermilk biscuits

Blend margarine, parsley flakes, dill weed, and onion in a 9-inch pie pan. Cut biscuits in quarters and dip each one in the margarine mixture. Arrange pieces touching in pie pan and bake in a 425 degree oven for 10 to 12 minutes, or until brown. Let stand a short time.

Delicious for luncheons or buffet dinners.

Shirley Tankersley
Ocilla, Georgia

QUICK ROLLS
(A first edition favorite)

1   package yeast
1   cup warm milk
3   tablespoons sugar
6   tablespoons oil
1½   teaspoon salt
2   cups all-purpose flour

Dissolve yeast in warm milk. Add sugar, oil and salt. Beat until smooth. Add flour to make soft dough. Knead, roll out, cut. Place on greased pan. Let rise 2 hours. Bake at 350 degrees for 15 to 20 minutes.

Carol Ann Morrison
Lumpkin, Georgia

BETTY'S ROLLS

(A first edition favorite)

1   package yeast
¼   cup lukewarm water
1   cup milk
¼   cup sugar
¼   cup shortening
1   teaspoon salt
1   egg, beaten
3½   cups all-purpose flour

Dissolve yeast in lukewarm water. Set in warm place. Scald milk; add sugar, shortening, and salt to milk, let cool. Add beaten egg and dissolved yeast to milk mixture. Sift 3½ cups plain flour. Add 2 cups to milk mixture. Gradually add remaining flour. Put in greased bowl and let rise until doubled in bulk, about 1½ to 2 hours. Knead for about 5 minutes. Refrigerate until ready to use. Cut or roll into shapes and brush with butter. Place in warm place until doubled. Bake at 350 – 400 degrees until brown.

Linda West
Byromville, Georgia

CHURCH BREAD

⅓   cup corn oil
2   cups self-rising corn meal mix
1¾   cups buttermilk
¼   cup corn oil

In a 10 x 2-inch iron skillet, pour about ⅓ cup oil. Mix meal, buttermilk and ¼ cup oil together. Mix well and pour into skillet. (There needs to be enough oil in the skillet to run up over the bread a little so you can grease the top.) Bake at 450 degrees for 20-25 minutes.

The oil on top of the bread gives it a crispy crust all over. This recipe is great for Thanksgiving dressing.

Nancy Coleman
Hartsfield, Georgia

BROCCOLI CORNBREAD

(A first edition favorite)

1	(10-ounce) package frozen chopped broccoli
1	medium onion, chopped
½	cup butter or margarine, melted
2	eggs, slightly beaten
1	cup sour cream, cottage cheese or plain yogurt
1	box Jiffy Mix cornbread mix

Cook broccoli according to package directions; drain. Spray a 9x13-inch pan with cooking spray; set aside. Prepare the Jiffy Mix cornbread mix according to the package directions, omitting the eggs. Add broccoli, onion, butter, eggs and sour cream. Mix together well. Pour mixture into the baking pan and bake at 375 degrees for 45-50 minutes. Cut into squares and serve immediately.

Charlotte Wingate
Doerun, Georgia

QUICK MEXICAN CORNBREAD

1	(8.5- ounce) package corn bread mix
1	(8-ounce) can cream-style corn
½	tablespoon finely chopped jalapeño peppers
1	cup sharp Cheddar cold pack cheese spread

Prepare corn bread as directed on package, adding corn and jalapeno peppers. Spread half the batter in greased 8-inch square pan. Dot with half the cheese. Add remaining batter, spreading evenly; dot with remaining cheese. Bake at 375 degrees for 25 minutes or until done. Cut into squares.

Mary Barber
Tifton, Georgia

MEXICAN CORNBREAD

1	cup cornmeal
1	(8 ¾- ounce) can cream-style corn
1	cup sour cream
½	cup oil
2	eggs, beaten
1	teaspoon salt
3	teaspoons baking powder
¼	cup hot pepper, finely chopped
½	cup bell pepper, finely chopped
1	cup grated sharp cheese

Mix together all ingredients, except pepper and cheese. Pour ½ batter in hot greased pan. Sprinkle pepper and cheese over batter; pour rest of batter on top of cheese and pepper. Bake 1 hour at 350 degrees.

Cassandra Bullington
Cordele, Georgia

QUICK GOOD CORNBREAD

1	cup self-rising cornmeal
1	(8-ounce) carton sour cream
1	(8½-ounce) can cream-style corn
½	cup vegetable oil
2	eggs, beaten

Combine all ingredients, mix well. Place in greased corn stick pan, muffin pan, or baking pan that has been preheated. Bake in 400 degree oven for 20 minutes or until light brown. Yields: 24 corn sticks, 16 muffins or 20 squares.

Shirley Tankersley
Ocilla, Georgia

ALMOND BISCOTTI

12   ounces (2 ½ cups) whole, shelled almonds, toasted
1¾   cups sugar
4   cups all-purpose flour
3   tablespoons unsweetened cocoa (optional)
2   teaspoons baking powder
½   teaspoon salt
6   eggs
3 - 6 tablespoons Amaretto almond liqueur
½   teaspoon pure almond extract
2   tablespoons melted butter

Preheat oven to 350 degrees. Butter a cookie sheet (airbake cookie sheet is best). Place half the nuts and all of the sugar in a blender or processor and process until the nuts are finely chopped; place in a bowl. Coarsely chop the remaining nuts and add to the bowl, along with the other dry ingredients. In a small bowl, blend the eggs, liqueur and butter. *Stir egg mixture into the dry ingredients and knead gently with your hands until incorporated. Divide the dough in half and form 2 loaves (spaced apart on respective sides of sheet – leave about an inch on the outer edges for spreading during baking). Make the loaves about 14 inches long x 3 inches wide x 1 inch high. Bake for 40 minutes and remove from the oven. Using an offset or straight cake spatula, carefully run it under each loaf to separate from the pan. Do not pry as it will damage the loaf. Cool biscotti for 10 minutes. Lower the oven temperature to 300 degrees. With a serrated bread knife, cut the loaves into about ½ inch slices (Use a towel if too hot to handle). Place biscotti back on cookie sheet, standing upright and spaced well apart. They should all fit on the one sheet, but the heat needs to circulate around each piece during the second baking. Bake for about another 20 minutes, until crisp and dry, but not browned on the bottoms. Cool completely and store in airtight container at room temperature. Though ready to eat with coffee, cocoa, tea, wine, milk or juice, chocolate may be melted in a double boiler and drizzled over the biscotti. Or dip the biscotti into the chocolate. Allow the chocolate to cool and set before handling. Yield: about 30 servings

*I pour the egg mixture and dry ingredients into my Kitchenaid mixer, loaded with a dough hook and let it do the kneading for me. Occasionally, I scrape the

sides with a sturdy, rubber spatula, making sure the bottom of the bowl is not hiding any unmixed ingredients. The dough is very sticky and rather tough to manipulate but it's worth the effort. I wet my hands for the next step to make it easier to handle the dough. Bon appetite… and don't forget to dunk!

Karen Nikitopoulos
Georgia Cotton Commission
Perry, Georgia

PECAN CRANBERRY BISCOTTI

1 ½	cups pecan halves, toasted
2	teaspoons baking powder
2 ½	cups all-purpose flour
1 ¼	cups sugar
⅛	teaspoon salt
3	large eggs
1	large egg yolk
3	tablespoons butter, softened
1	teaspoon vanilla extract
1	cup dried cranberries

Zest of 1 lemon

Heat oven to 350 degrees. Finely chop pecans; set aside. In an electric mixer fitted with the paddle attachment, combine baking powder, flour, sugar and salt. In a bowl, beat eggs, yolks, and vanilla. Add to dry ingredients; mix on medium low until sticky dough is formed. Stir in pecans, cranberries and lemon zest. Turn dough out onto well-floured board; sprinkle with flour, and knead slightly. Shape into 9 x 3½ inch logs. Transfer to prepared baking sheet. Bake until golden brown, 25 to 30 minutes. Let cool enough to handle, about 10 minutes. Reduce oven to 275 degrees. On cutting board, cut logs on diagonal into ½ -inch-thick slices. Return pieces cut side down to baking sheet. Bake until lightly toasted, about 20 minutes. Turn over. Bake until slightly dry, about 20 minutes. Cool on wire rack. Store in airtight container.

Very good!

Jane Gibbs
Moultrie, Georgia

MOTHER'S LACEY HOE-CAKES

1	cup fine ground plain white cornmeal
½	teaspoon salt
¼	teaspoon soda
½	teaspoon peanut oil
½	cup milk
½	cup peanut oil

Mix cornmeal, salt, soda and ½ teaspoon oil, adding milk until quite thin. Heat ½ cup peanut oil in iron skillet until water sprinkled on skillet bounces. Drop cornmeal mixture by tablespoon into hot oil. Turn when brown and crisp. Drain on paper towel and serve hot. Yield: 4-6 servings

My mother, Edith Stripling, made these for our family from our childhood until her death in May, 2008. She was a fabulous old-fashioned cook who loved to cook for her family. She grew up during the depression and had to make-do with few ingredients, but she could make some delicious meals. She was a wonderful mother and I miss her so much.

Charlotte Mathis
Moultrie, Georgia

Cotton was first planted in Georgia in the Trustees Garden in Savannah in 1733 with seed from England. Though cotton was grown in other colonies, Georgia was the first colony to produce it for commercial purposes.

GRILLED TEX-MEX TOAST

½	cup butter, melted
1	teaspoon cumin
1	teaspoon dried oregano
½	teaspoon paprika
8	dashes hot red pepper sauce or to taste
⅛	teaspoon salt
8	slices Texas Toast or BBQ bread

Combine butter, cumin, oregano, paprika and hot pepper sauce in small bowl. Brush over both sides of bread slices. Lightly grease grill grid. Place bread on grid over medium coals. Grill 1 to 2 minutes on each side or until toasted. Watch carefully to prevent burning. To use a grill pan, heat grill pan over medium heat until hot. Grill prepared bread 5 minutes on each side until toasted.

Great for a summertime barbecue.

Nancy Coleman
Hartsfield, Georgia

BACON CHEESE MUFFINS

1	cup self-rising flour
1	stick butter or margarine, softened
1	cup (8 ounces) sour cream
¾	cup cooked crumbled bacon (about ½ pound)
¾	cup grated sharp Cheddar cheese

Mix together softened butter and sour cream. Add flour. Stir in cheese and crumbled bacon. Fill sprayed mini muffin tins two-thirds full. Bake at 350 degrees. Check after 15 minutes but they usually need 20 minutes. Should be light brown, no burned cheese. Yield: 24-30 muffins depending on size of muffin tins.

Virginia Hart
Moultrie, Georgia

SOUR CREAM ROLLS

½   cup (1 stick) butter, melted
1   (8-ounce) carton sour cream
2   cups biscuit mix

Let butter cool after melting. Stir in sour cream; add biscuit mix. Put in well greased or buttered muffin pans. Cook at 350 degrees for 25 minutes. Makes 12 rolls.

Chris Loraine, Moultrie, Georgia
Tonya Loraine Bustle, Coolidge, Georgia

MONKEY BREAD

(A first edition favorite)

Mixture A:
1   cup sugar
1   tablespoon cinnamon
1   cup chopped nuts (optional)
Mixture B:
½   cup (1 stick) butter, melted
1   cup brown sugar
1   tablespoon cinnamon
1   package frozen yeast rolls (You can substitute 4 cans of biscuits [10 each] for the yeast rolls, but the yeast rolls are better.)

Thaw yeast rolls enough to be able to cut into fourths. Roll the yeast balls in mixture A until well coated. Place them in a greased tube or Bundt pan. Pour left over mixture on top of balls. Put mixture B into the microwave until butter is melted. Stir the butter, brown sugar and cinnamon until blended. Pour this mixture over the yeast rolls in the tube pan. Take a knife and allow this mixture to go between the yeast balls. Let rise to fill the pan (or leave out on the counter over night). Bake at 350 degrees for 30 to 35 minutes.

This recipe has __no__ calories! This is a favorite of young and old. Great with your morning coffee.

Nancy Coleman
Hartsfield, Georgia

QUICK MONKEY BREAD

4 cans biscuits (40 biscuits)
1 ⅔ cup sugar
2 teaspoons cinnamon
½ cup chopped nuts
1 ½ sticks margarine
½ cup raisins

Cut each biscuit into 4 pieces. Roll the biscuit pieces in a mixture of ⅔ cup sugar and 1 teaspoon cinnamon. Put ½ the pieces in bottom of ungreased Bundt pan. Boil margarine, 1 cup sugar and 1 teaspoon of cinnamon for two minutes. Pour half over this mixture over first layer of biscuits. Add nuts and raisins. Top with the remaining biscuit pieces (rolled in cinnamon and sugar mixture). Top with the rest of the syrup mixture. Bake for 30 minutes at 350 degrees. Take out of pan immediately.

This is very good for breakfast.

Cassandra Bullington
Cordele, Georgia

PECAN PIE MINI MUFFINS

1 cup light brown sugar
½ cup all-purpose flour
2 eggs, beaten
⅔ cup melted butter
1 cup chopped pecans

Preheat oven to 350 degrees. Mix all ingredients in a bowl with a wooden spoon. Pour into mini muffin tins, sprayed with cooking spray, and fill each half full. Place a pecan half on each. Bake 12 - 15 minutes. Yield: approximately 3 dozen

Cathy Thompson
Vienna, Georgia

MAGIC MARSHMALLOWS PUFFS
(A first edition favorite)

1   (8-ounce) can crescent dinner rolls
8   large marshmallows
2   tablespoons sugar
1   teaspoon cinnamon
Melted margarine

Unroll crescent rolls into 8 triangles. Mix cinnamon and sugar. Dip marshmallows in butter and then in cinnamon-sugar. Place one marshmallow on the short side of each roll. Stretch corner of dough over marshmallow and roll towards opposite point, completely covering marshmallow; seal edges well. Dip in margarine and place in muffin tins. Bake at 375 degrees for 11 to 15 minutes or until golden brown. Immediately remove from pan. Cool slightly.

Glaze:
⅓   cup powdered sugar
1   to 2 teaspoons milk
¼   teaspoon vanilla

In small bowl, combine glaze ingredients; mix well. Drizzle over warm puffs.
Yield: 8 puffs

Variation:
Use half of a snack-size candy bar (preferably with chewy or nougat center) instead of marshmallow. Don't use cinnamon-sugar mixture. Glaze with ½ cup powdered sugar and 2 teaspoons cocoa dissolved in 3 to 4 teaspoons milk.

Children (and adults) love to make (and eat) these. What's the magic? This marshmallow disappears!

Nancy Coleman
Hartsfield, Georgia

PECAN PIE MUFFINS

1   cup chopped pecans
½   cup all-purpose flour
1   cup light brown sugar
2   eggs
½   cup melted butter

Mix first 3 ingredients together. Add eggs and butter. Stir just until mixed. Line muffin pans with paper baking cups. Fill muffin liners with mixture. Bake 350 degrees for 20-22 minutes. Yield: Makes about 10 large muffins or 24 small ones.

Very easy—very good!!!

Gail Thompson
Moultrie, Georgia

PETITE CINNAMON ROLLS

1   (8-ounce) package refrigerated crescent rolls
2   tablespoons butter or margarine, softened
2   tablespoons sugar
½   teaspoon ground cinnamon
2   tablespoons raisins (optional)

Glaze:
¾   cup powdered sugar
2-3 teaspoons milk

Preheat over to 350 degrees. For cinnamon rolls, unroll crescent dough into 1 large rectangle; press perforations together with fingers to seal. Spread butter evenly over dough. In small bowl, combine sugar and cinnamon; sprinkle evenly over dough. Top with raisins, if desired. Start at longest side, roll up in jelly-roll fashion; press edges together to seal. Cut crosswise into 20 slices. Place slices, cut side down, in greased 8-inch round cake pan. Bake 20-25 minutes or until golden brown. Cool 5-10 minutes. For glaze, stir together powdered sugar and milk in small bowl until smooth. Drizzle over warm rolls. Yield: 20 rolls

Virginia Hart
Moultrie, Georgia

SPICED PUMPKIN NUT BREAD

4	cups all-purpose flour
1	tablespoon pumpkin pie spice
2	teaspoons baking powder
1	teaspoon baking soda
¾	teaspoon salt
1	(15-ounce) can pure pumpkin
2	cups packed brown sugar
1	cup apple juice
4	large eggs
¼	cup vegetable oil
2	teaspoons vanilla extract
1	cup chopped nuts, divided

Preheat over to 350 degrees. Grease two 9x5-inch loaf pans. Sift flour, pumpkin pie spice, baking powder, baking soda and salt into a medium bowl. Combine pumpkin, sugar, juice, eggs, oil and vanilla in a large bowl; stir well. Stir in flour mixture and ¾ cup nuts just until moistened. Spoon into prepared loaf pans. Sprinkle remaining nuts over top of loaves. Bake 60-70 minutes or until wooden pick inserted in center comes out clean. Cool in pans on wire racks for 10 minutes; remove to wire racks to cool completely.

Vickie Abrams
Berlin, Georgia

The Boll Weevil Eradication Program was implemented in Georgia in 1987. It has lowered production costs, provided conditions for an increased yield of cotton per acre, and reduced the use of pesticides in cotton production by 90 percent.

Breads

APPLE BREAD

½	cup vegetable oil
3	eggs
2	cups sugar
3	cups all-purpose flour
1	cup chopped toasted pecans
2	teaspoons baking soda
1	teaspoons salt
1	teaspoon vanilla extract
3	cups apples, coarsely chopped

Mix oil, eggs and sugar; add remaining ingredients. Pour into 2 small 8x4-inch loaf pans that have been slightly greased and floured. Bake at 350 degrees for 90 minutes. Top with glaze while warm.

Glaze:

½	cup (1 stick) butter
1	cup sugar
½	cup evaporated milk

Bring all ingredients to a boil in a small saucepan. Pour over baked bread.

Angela Gibbs White
Pearson, Georgia

CRANBERRY BREAD

2   cups all purpose flour, sifted
1   cup sugar
1 ½   teaspoons baking powder
½   teaspoon soda
1   teaspoon salt
¾   cup orange juice
1   tablespoon grated orange rind
¼   cup of shortening
1   egg, well beaten
½   cup chopped nuts
1 ½   cups fresh or frozen cranberries, chopped

Sift together flour, sugar, baking powder, soda, and salt. Cut in shortening until mixture resembles coarse corn meal. Combine orange juice and grated rind with egg. Pour all at once into dry ingredients, mixing just enough to dampen. Fold in chopped nuts and berries. (If berries are frozen, do not thaw chop frozen.) Spoon into greased 9x5x3-inch loaf pan and bake at 350 degrees about 1 hour or until golden brown.

Mary Walker
Tifton, Georgia

CREAM CHEESE DANISH WITH GLAZE

2	(8-ounce) packages crescent dinner rolls
2	(8-ounce) packages cream cheese
½	cup sugar
1	egg yolk
1	egg white
1	teaspoon vanilla extract
2	teaspoons fresh lemon juice

Glaze:

2	teaspoons margarine, melted
1	cup powdered sugar

In a 9x13-inch pan, press one pack of dinner rolls to cover bottom of pan. Mix cream cheese, sugar, egg yolk, vanilla and lemon juice until smooth. Spread over dinner rolls. Unroll second package of dinner rolls and cover the cream cheese mixture. Beat egg white and brush over dinner rolls. Bake at 350 degrees for 25 minutes. Remove from oven and allow to cool for 10 minutes. Mix margarine and sugar together. Add enough water to make it spreadable. Spread over baked pastry. Cut into small squares before serving. Danish cuts best when it is thoroughly cooled, like the next day.

Jane Gibbs
Moultrie, Georgia

CREAM CHEESE DANISH

2	(8-ounce) packages cream cheese
1 ½	cups sugar (divided)
1	egg (separate yolk from white)
1	teaspoon vanilla
1	tablespoon cinnamon
2	tubes of crescent rolls

In an ungreased rectangular casserole dish, layer one tube of crescent rolls and press seams together. Cream together the 2 packages of cream cheese, 1 cup of sugar, the egg yolk, and vanilla and spread over the crescent rolls. Top with the second tube of crescent rolls. Lightly beat the egg white and brush over the top layer of crescent rolls. Combine ½ cup sugar and cinnamon and sprinkle on top. Bake for 20-25 minutes at 375 degrees. Can be served as a breakfast pastry or topped with ice cream for a dessert.

Mary B. Smith
Brinson, Georgia

STRAWBERRY DANISH

1	package hot roll mix
²/₃	cup very warm water (105-115 degrees)
2	tablespoons sugar
½	cup firm margarine or butter
1	egg, beaten
½	cup finely chopped nuts
½	cup golden raisins
¾	cup strawberry preserves
1	cup powdered sugar
4-5	tablespoons milk

In a large bowl, dissolve yeast from hot roll mix in water. In medium-size bowl, combine flour mixture from hot roll mix and sugar. Cut in firm margarine until mixture has particles the size of peas. Combine with yeast mixture. Add egg; blend well. Cover; let rise in a warm place until light and doubled in size, about 1 hour. In small bowl, combine nuts, raisins and preserves; set aside. Punch down dough. Knead on floured surface until no longer sticky, about 1 minute. Roll out dough to 16x12-inch rectangle. Spread with filling. Starting with 16-inch side roll up tightly; seal edge. Cut roll in half crosswise forming 8-inch rolls. Cut each roll almost through in half lengthwise. Place one roll on large ungreased cookie sheet; gently spread apart to form flat coffee cake. Repeat with remaining roll, placing at least 2-inches from other coffee cake. Cover; let rise in warm place until light and doubled in size, 45 to 60 minutes. Heat oven to 350 degrees. Bake 25 to 30 minutes or until golden brown. Immediately remove from cookie sheet. Cool slightly. Combine powdered sugar and milk; drizzle over coffee cake.

Vickie Abrams
Berlin, Georgia

Breads

Cakes and Frostings

ANTEBELLUM COTTON

The invention of the cotton gin in 1793 and the construction of the first textile mill in Georgia in 1811, combined with demand from English mills, led to the expansion of cotton acreage. By the 1820's, cotton production was beginning to change the agricultural pattern in Georgia which had been dominated by small farmers. Production increased from 1,000 bales in 1790 to 90,000 bales in 1820. By 1826, Georgia was the leading cotton state, producing 150,000 bales.

Cotton so dominated farming in the state that farmers were growing cotton instead of grain and other crops, choosing to buy those crops from Midwestern states. The practice of crop rotation had not been developed and the land was beginning to show fatigue. The economy of the state had become contingent on the success or failure of the cotton crop.

During the 1840's the winds of war had begun to blow. State leaders pushed for diversification so that the state would not be dependent on the North for its food or to produce finished goods from the cotton. Because of the profitability of cotton, producers were not willing to diversify. Demand for cotton continued to grow. By 1850, cotton approached its pinnacle as "king." It was everywhere with more than one-third of the cropland, a half million acres, devoted to cotton. By 1860, it was generating $30,000,000.

INDEX

Cakes and Frostings

SOCK-IT-TO-ME CAKE

Cake

1	package butter recipe cake mix
1	cup sour cream
½	cup oil
¼	cup sugar
¼	cup water
4	eggs

Filling

1	cup chopped pecans
2	tablespoons brown sugar
2	teaspoons cinnamon

Glaze

1	cup powdered sugar
4	teaspoons water or milk

In large mixing bowl, blend cake mix, sour cream, oil, sugar, water and eggs. Beat at high speed for 2 minutes. Pour two-thirds of the batter into a greased and floured 10-inch tube pan. Combine filling ingredients and sprinkle over batter in pan. Spread remaining batter evenly over filling mixture. Gently swirl filling and batter. Bake 375 degrees for 45 to 55 minutes. Cool in pan for 15 minutes. Whisk glaze ingredients together. Remove cake from pan and drizzle with glaze.

I've been making this cake since the 1970's. No one says "sock-it-to-me" anymore, but we're still eating this cake. Great with coffee.

Lois Clark
Cairo, Georgia

 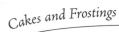

GRANDMA THOMPSON'S ORANGE SLICE CAKE

(A first edition favorite)

1	cup butter
2	cups sugar
4	eggs
1	teaspoon baking soda
½	cup buttermilk
3 ½	cups all-purpose flour
1	box dates, cut in small pieces
1	can flake coconut
2	cups chopped nuts
1	(1-pound) package orange slice candy

Cream butter and sugar. Add eggs one at a time. Dissolve baking soda in buttermilk. Add flour alternately with buttermilk. Roll nuts, orange slice candy, and dates in small amount of flour. Add nut mixture to cake batter along with coconut. Bake in a greased tube pan at 250 degrees for 2 to 2 ½ hours. Do not remove from pan.

Orange Glaze:

1	cup orange juice (fresh or frozen)
2	cups powdered sugar

Mix well, pour over cake as soon as taken from oven. LET CAKE STAND IN PAN OVERNIGHT.

Grandma made this cake every Christmas. It was Georgia Farmers Market Bulletin Recipe of the Week.

Gail Thompson
Moultrie, Georgia

Cakes and Frostings

FRANKLIN NUT CAKE

(A first-edition favorite)

1	pound butter (margarine will do, but not as flavorful)
2	cups sugar
6	eggs
4	cups all-purpose flour
1	teaspoons baking powder
¼	teaspoon salt
1	cup (½ pound) candied cherries
1	cup (½ pound) candied pineapple
1	pound (2 to 4 cups) pecans
1	teaspoon vanilla extract
1	teaspoon butter flavoring
1	teaspoon lemon extract

Cream butter and sugar. Add beaten eggs. Add 3 cups flour with baking powder and salt. Mix remaining cup of flour with fruit and nuts. Stir into batter. Add vanilla and other flavorings. Pour into tube pan that has been greased and lined with brown paper (grocery bag is good). Bake at 250 degrees for 3 hours. Let cool in pan.

This is a cake I've made for many years. We enjoy it better than fruit cake. I make one at Thanksgiving and a couple during Christmas holidays.

Yvonne Crawford
Chula, Georgia

When baking, don't use reduced fat or soft butter or margarine. They have a higher water content which diminishes the quality of baked goods.

FRESH APPLE SPICE CAKE

Cake:

1	cup vegetable oil
2	cups sugar
3	eggs
3	cups all-purpose flour
1	teaspoon soda
¼	teaspoon salt
1	teaspoon nutmeg
1	teaspoon cinnamon
1	teaspoon vanilla extract
1	cup chopped nuts
3	cups peeled and finely-chopped apples

Glaze:

½	cup sugar
¼	cup buttermilk
¼	teaspoon soda
2	tablespoons margarine
1½	teaspoon vanilla extract

Combine oil and sugar; beat well. Add eggs, one at a time, beating well after each addition. Combine flour, soda, salt, cinnamon and nutmeg; stir. Add dry ingredients to sugar mixture, beating well. Add vanilla; mix well. Stir in nuts and apples. Pour batter into a greased and floured 10-inch tube pan. Bake at 350 degrees for 1 hour and 15 minutes or until cake tests done. Using a toothpick, punch holes in cake while hot; spoon glaze over cake. Cool. Remove from pan.

Glaze: Combine all ingredients in a medium saucepan. Bring to a boil and boil 4 minutes, stirring occasionally.

This is a very good cake, but wait until the following day to eat. The longer it stands, the moister it gets.

Vickie Hart Abrams
Berlin, Georgia

LITTLE DIXIE POUND CAKE

3   tablespoons real butter, (not margarine), softened
6   tablespoons sugar
1   egg
6   tablespoons all-purpose flour
Pinch of baking soda
7   teaspoons buttermilk
¼   teaspoon vanilla extract
⅛   teaspoon orange extract

In a small bowl, cream butter and sugar. Beat in egg. Combine flour and baking soda; add alternately with buttermilk to creamed mixture. Blend in vanilla and orange extracts. Pour into a greased 5¾ x 3 x 2-inch loaf pan. Bake at 350 degrees for 30-35 minutes or until cake tests done. Cool for 10 minutes. Remove from pan and cool on rack.

Mary Hart Braswell
Berlin, Georgia

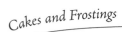

CHOCOLATE BUTTERMILK POUND CAKE

½   pound (2 sticks) butter
½   cup shortening
3   cups sugar
5   large eggs
1   cup buttermilk
3   cups flour
½   teaspoon salt
¼   teaspoon baking powder
1   teaspoon vanilla extract

Cream butter and shortening until light and fluffy. Add sugar slowly and beat well until creamy. Add eggs one at a time, beating well after each. Sift together flour, salt, and baking powder. Add dry ingredients alternately with buttermilk to the mixture. Add vanilla flavoring and blend. Pour batter into greased and floured Bundt pan. Bake at 325 degrees for 1 hour or longer. Remove from oven. Allow to cool in pan for 10 minutes. Remove from pan. Pour frosting over cake.

Frosting:
2   cups powdered sugar
¼   cup cocoa
4   tablespoons evaporated milk
2   tablespoons butter

Place all ingredients in saucepan until melted, but do not boil.

Gail Thompson
Moultrie, Georgia

Cakes and Frostings

IRMA'S WHIPPING CREAM POUND CAKE

(A first edition favorite)

2 ¾   cups sugar
1 ½   cups shortening
6   eggs
3   cups cake flour, sifted
1   (8-ounce) carton whipping cream (do not whip)
Dash of salt
2   teaspoons vanilla extract
2   teaspoons lemon extract

Cream sugar and shortening together. Add eggs one at a time. Beat well. Add a little flour and a little whipping cream until you have used all flour and cream. Start and end with flour. Add salt and extracts. Bake at 325 degrees for 1 hour and 15 minutes. Check for doneness. Cool in pan for 15 minutes. Remove from pan cool on rack top side up or down, depending on your preference.

A very moist cake. This recipe is from my husband's grandmother, Irma Davis Coleman, a cotton woman from years past. Great straight from the oven or served with fresh strawberries or with ambrosia at Christmas or Thanksgiving.

Nancy Coleman,
Hartsfield, Georgia

WHIPPING CREAM POUND CAKE

2   sticks butter
3   cups sugar
3   cups cake flour
6   eggs
½   pint whipping cream
2   teaspoons vanilla

Cream butter and sugar. Add eggs, one at a time, beating well after each addition. Add the whipping cream and flour alternately while blending. Add vanilla and continue to blend. Pour into greased and floured tube pan and bake at 300 degrees for 1½ hours. Do NOT preheat oven.

Kim Miller Thompson
Dalton, Georgia

AUNT NELDA'S POUND CAKE

½ pound (2 sticks) butter
3 cups granulated sugar, sifted
6 eggs
3 cups cake flour
½ pint (8 ounces) whipping cream
2 teaspoons vanilla extract

Cream together butter and sugar, adding eggs, one at a time. Add flour and cream, alternating; add vanilla. Pour into a greased tube pan. Bump pan before putting in oven. Bake at 300 degrees for 1 ½ hours or until pick inserted comes out clean. Cool 10 minutes in pan before removing.

Delicious! And yes, you do sift the sugar.

Brenda Morris,
Ocilla, Georgia

POPPY SEED CAKE

1 box yellow cake mix
1 large box French Vanilla instant pudding mix
4 eggs
1 (8-ounce) carton sour cream
½ cup oil
½ cup crème sherry wine
⅓ cup poppy seed

Mix cake mix and pudding mix; add eggs one at a time. Add sour cream, oil, wine and poppy seeds and beat 5 minutes. Spray Bundt pan. Pour batter into pan. Bake 350 degrees 45 to 50 minutes. Cool in pan for 15 minutes before removing.

Brenda Morris
Ocilla, Georgia

Cakes and Frostings

COCONUT CAKE

1	cup (2 sticks) margarine
1 ¾	cups sugar
5	eggs
2 ¾	cups flour
3	teaspoons baking powder
½	teaspoon salt
½	cup milk or coconut milk
½	teaspoon lemon extract (optional) or 1 teaspoon vanilla extract

Preheat oven to 350 degrees. Sift together flour, baking powder and salt. Cream margarine and gradually add sugar. Add eggs one at a time beating well after each addition. Add flour mixture alternately with milk, beginning and ending with flour. Add lemon extract. Bake 25 to 30 minutes in 3 or 4 pans which have been greased, floured and lined with wax or parchment paper. Makes four large layers.

Filling:

2	cups milk		2	cups sugar
½	cup (1 stick) margarine		½	fresh coconut, grated

Combine milk, sugar, and margarine in a saucepan. Cook until thick enough to stay on cake (about 220 degrees). This takes a long time. Cool. (This takes a long time, too. Put saucepan in refrigerator and forget it for a while.) When cool and thick enough to stay on cake, add three-fourths of the coconut. Save remainder of coconut to put on top of cake. Spread between layers of cake. Frost tops and sides with White Boiled Frosting. Sprinkle top and sides with remaining coconut.

White Boiled Frosting:

2	cups sugar		2	egg whites
½	cup cold water		1	teaspoon vinegar
½	teaspoon vanilla extract		1	teaspoon baking powder

Beat egg whites until stiff. Cook sugar, water and vinegar until it spins a long thread. Slowly pour over egg whites. Add baking powder and vanilla. Spread on top and sides of cake and sprinkle with coconut. This icing is firm but not hard so it makes slicing the cake easier. A great icing for birthday cakes.

This is the recipe I use for my Christmas cake. Makes a very large, beautiful and delicious cake. I got the recipe from the Atlanta Journal, Christmas 1964.

Lois Clark
Cairo, Georgia

Cakes and Frostings

ITALIAN CREAM CAKE

(or *Butternut Cake*) *(A first edition favorite)*

½	cup (1 stick) margarine	1	cup buttermilk
½	cup shortening	1	teaspoon vanilla extract
2	cups sugar	1	cup chopped nuts
5	egg yolks	1	(7-ounce) package coconut
2	cups flour	5	egg whites, stiffly beaten
1	teaspoon soda		

Preheat oven to 350 degrees. Grease and flour three cake pans. Line bottom with wax paper. Cream margarine and shortening; add sugar and beat until mixture is smooth. Add egg yolks and beat well. Combine flour and soda and add to creamed mixture alternately with buttermilk. Stir in vanilla. Add coconut and chopped nuts. Fold in stiffly beaten egg whites. Pour batter into prepared pans. Bake for 25 minutes or until cake tests done; cool in pans for 5 minutes and turn out on racks to cool completely.

Cream Cheese Frosting
- 1 ½ (8-ounce) packages cream cheese
- 6 tablespoons (3/4 stick) margarine
- 6 cups powdered sugar, sifted
- 1½ teaspoons vanilla extract
- Chopped pecans
- Coconut (optional)

Beat cream cheese and margarine until smooth; add sugar and mix well. Add vanilla, nuts and coconut. Spread between layers and on top and sides of cake. Sprinkle top with pecans.

Butternut Variation: Substitute 3 teaspoons butternut flavoring for vanilla in both cake and frosting.

I use four layers; three are very thick. I also put both coconut and nuts in the frosting.

Nancy Coleman
Hartsfield, Georgia

When using coconut in a cake batter, process coconut in blender or food processor until coarsely chopped. This will make the cake easier to cut.

Cakes and Frostings

IRISH CREAM CAKE

Cake:
>   White cake mix with pudding in mix
>   Ingredients listed on cake mix box
>   2   tablespoons instant coffee

Mix cake according to directions using hot water in which the instant coffee has been dissolved. Bake in three 9-inch round greased and floured cake pans. Bake according to package directions. Cool in pans on racks for 10 minutes. Invert on cooling racks and remove pans; cool completely.

Frosting:
>   1   cup (2 sticks) butter or margarine, softened
>   ¼   cup Baileys Irish Cream liqueur
>   1 ½ tablespoons instant coffee
>   4   cups powdered sugar, sifted
>   2   (6-ounce) packages slivered almonds, toasted

Dissolve instant coffee in liqueur; set aside until completely dissolved. Cream butter in large mixing bowl. Gradually blend in powdered sugar. Add Irish Cream/coffee mixture and beat until creamy. Spread between layers, on top and sides of cake. Cover top and sides with toasted almonds. Yield: 12-16 servings

Delicious and I don't even like coffee.

Nancy Coleman
Hartsfield, Georgia

FAT GRANNY'S RED VELVET CAKE

2 ½   cups self-rising flour
2 ¼   ounces red food color
1   cup buttermilk
1 ½   cups sugar
1 ½   cups vegetable oil
1   teaspoon cocoa
1   teaspoon baking soda (add last)
1   teaspoon white vinegar
1   teaspoon vanilla extract
2   large eggs

Mix self-rising flour, red food coloring, buttermilk, sugar, vegetable oil, cocoa, white vinegar, vanilla extract, eggs and baking soda. Pour in three 9-inch greased cake pans and bake at 350 degrees for 18-20 minutes or until tests done.

Frosting:
½   pound (2 sticks) butter
8   ounces cream cheese
1   (1 pound) box powdered sugar
1   cup nuts, chopped

Cream butter, cream cheese and sugar together. Frost cake. Add nuts after icing cake. Refrigerate cake.

Mary Barber
Tifton, Georgia

From New York to California, denim continues to drive consumer demand for cotton. Creative and marketable finishing processes – like stone-washed jeans and wrinkle-free cotton fabrics – offer consumers more choices and more reasons to buy cotton.

CREAM CARAMEL CAKE

1   cup (2 sticks) butter (I sometimes use 1 stick of butter and 1 of margarine)
3   cups granulated sugar
6   eggs
2 ⅔ cups all-purpose flour
½   teaspoon baking soda
1   teaspoon salt
1   cup sour cream
1   tablespoon vanilla extract

Preheat oven to 350 degrees. Grease and flour 4 or 6 9-inch cake pans. Cream butter first. Add sugar and cream until fluffy. Add eggs, one at a time, beating well after each addition. Sift flour and measure. Add baking soda and salt to sifted flour. Alternately add flour and sour cream to butter mixture, beginning and ending with flour. Add vanilla. Pour into 4 or 6 prepared cake pans. If using 4 pans, bake for 25 minutes. If using 6 pans, bake for 20 minutes. Test for doneness. Remove from oven and cool on racks for 10 minutes. Carefully remove from pans to cool completely. Frost.

Caramel Frosting:
1   cup (2 sticks) butter
1 ½ cups light brown sugar
½   cup dark brown sugar
½   cup evaporated milk
4   cups powdered sugar, sifted

Melt butter; add brown sugars and evaporated milk. Cook two minutes over medium heat, stirring constantly. Remove from heat. Add vanilla and pour over powdered sugar. Beat until smooth. Let cool slightly. Spread frosting between layers, on top and sides of cake.

Jane Grogan Gibbs
Moultrie, Georgia

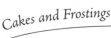
Cakes and Frostings

BASIC YELLOW CAKE

4	cups all-purpose or cake flour, sifted
4	teaspoons baking powder
1	cup butter
2	cups granulated sugar
1 ½	teaspoon vanilla extract
4	eggs
2	cups milk

Grease and flour four cake pans; line bottom with wax or parchment paper. In a large mixing bowl, cream the butter, sugar and vanilla. Add eggs, one at a time, beating thoroughly after each addition. Stir in the flour mixture in four additions, alternately with milk, just until smooth, beginning and ending with flour mixture. Turn into prepared pans. Bake at 350 degrees for 20 to 25 minutes or until cake tester inserted in the center comes out clean. Place cakes in pans on wire racks to cool for 5 minutes. Turn out on wire racks, turn right side up. Cool completely before frosting.

I used this recipe when I was teaching foods. A good basic cake recipe. Especially good with caramel or chocolate frosting.

Nancy Coleman
Hartsfield, Georgia

Cake flour has a lower protein content than all-purpose flour and produces a tender, delicate texture to a cake. Substitute all-purpose flour for cake flour by using 2 tablespoons less all-purpose flour per cup of cake flour. Cake flour should be sifted before measuring.

Cakes and Frostings

KEY LIME CAKE

Cake:
¾	cup oil
¾	cup orange juice
5	eggs
1	(3-ounce) box lime gelatin
1	box lemon cake mix

Preheat oven to 350 degrees. Mix ingredients according to cake mix directions. Bake in three greased and floured cake pans for 25-30 minutes until done. (Don't brown.) Cool in pans for 10 minutes. Remove from pans and allow to cool before frosting.

Lime Sugar Syrup:
6	tablespoons powdered sugar, sifted
¼	cup Key lime juice

Add juice to sugar and mix until smooth. Prick frosting layers with fork. Brush syrup over layers and allow to soak in.

Key Lime Buttercream Frosting:
1	cup (2 sticks) margarine, softened
2	(1-pound) boxes powdered sugar, sifted
1	tablespoon grated lime zest
⅓	cup Key lime juice

Additional grated lime zest for garnish, if desired

Blend margarine until creamy. Gradually add sugar. Blend in Key lime juice and lime zest. Spread between layers and on top and sides of cake. Garnish with additional grated lime zest, but take note: the zest will turn brown over time. Consider adding lime zest garnish just before serving.

Nancy Coleman
Hartsfield, Georgia

ORANGE PINEAPPLE DREAM CAKE

1	box yellow or white cake mix
1	(3-ounce) package vanilla instant pudding mix
1	cup oil
3	eggs
1	(11-ounce) can Mandarin oranges and juice

Combine all ingredients and beat 2 minutes. Grease and flour 3 cake pans. Pour batter into pans; bake at 325 degrees until light brown and cake begins to full away from sides of pan. Allow to cool in pans for 10 minutes. Remove from pans and cool.

Frosting:

1	(3-ounce) package vanilla instant pudding mix
1	(20-ounce) can crushed pineapple and juice
1	(9-ounce) carton whipped topping
	Coconut or pecans for garnish

Combine pudding mix with pineapple and juice. Beat 2 minutes. Fold in whipped topping. Frost cake. Garnish with coconut or pecans.

Vickie Abrams,
Berlin, Georgia

The first commercially grown cotton in Georgia was Sea Island cotton, an extra-long, silky fiber, planted in 1778. It was soon surpassed in commercial production by another native American species, Upland cotton, which today represents about 95% of U.S. production.

Cakes and Frostings

STRAWBERRY CAKE

1	box white cake mix
1	(3-ounce) box strawberry gelatin
4	eggs
½	cup water
½	cup (1 stick) butter

Mix cake mix, gelatin, eggs, water and butter; beat well. Bake in 3 prepared pans at 350° for 20 minutes.

Frosting

1	(1-pound) box powdered sugar	Red food coloring
½	cup frozen strawberries	

Mix powdered sugar and frozen strawberries. Add 3 drops of red food coloring. Spread over cake after it has cooled.

Mary Barber
Tifton, Georgia

JACKIE'S STRAWBERRY CAKE

1	box yellow cake mix	4	large eggs
1 ¼	cups milk	⅓	cup oil

Mix according to directions on box. Pour into three greased and floured 9-inch cake pans. Bake at 350 degrees for 18 to 20 minutes or until tests done.

Icing

1	(8-ounce) carton whipped topping
1	(8-ounce) carton sour cream
1	(1 pound) box powdered sugar
1	(8-ounce) package cream cheese
3	pints strawberries, sliced
½	cup sugar

Add ½ cup sugar to sliced strawberries; set aside. Mix whipping topping, sour cream, powdered sugar, and cream cheese. Layer icing and strawberries on cake. This will make a three-layer cake.

Jackie Rogers
Ochlocknee, Georgia

PRALINE-PUMPKIN TORTE

¾   cup brown sugar
⅓   cup butter or margarine
3   tablespoons whipping cream
¾   cup chopped pecans
3   large eggs
1 ⅔ cups sugar
1   cup vegetable oil
1   (15-ounce) can pumpkin
¼   teaspoon vanilla extract
2   cups all-purpose flour
2   teaspoons baking powder
2   teaspoons pumpkin pie spice
1   teaspoon baking soda
1   teaspoon salt
1   (8-ounce) carton whipped topping
Chopped pecans

Cook brown sugar, butter and whipping cream in a sauce pan over low heat, stirring until sugar dissolves. Pour into two greased 9-inch round cake pans; sprinkle evenly with ¾ cup pecans. Cool. Beat eggs, sugar, and oil at medium speed with an electric mixer. Add pumpkin and vanilla; beat well. Combine flour, baking powder, pumpkin pie spice, baking soda and salt; add to pumpkin mixture, beating until blended. Spoon batter evenly into prepared cake pans. Bake at 350 degrees for 30 to 35 minutes or until wooden pick inserted in center comes out clean. Cool cake layers in pans on wire racks 5 minutes; remove from pans, and cool on wire racks. Place one cake layer on a serving plate, praline side up; spread evenly with whipped cream topping. Top with remaining layer, praline side up, and spread remaining whipped cream topping over top of cake. Sprinkle cake with chopped pecans. Store in refrigerator.

Brenda Morris
Ocilla, Georgia

PRALINE TURTLE CAKE

½ cup butter or margarine
1 cup brown sugar
1 (14-ounce) can sweetened condensed milk
1 cup chopped pecans
2 cups all-purpose flour
¾ cup unsweetened cocoa
2 cups granulated sugar
1 ½ teaspoon baking powder
1 ½ teaspoon baking soda

1 teaspoon salt
2 large eggs
1 cup sour cream
½ cup oil
1 teaspoon vanilla extract
1 teaspoon white vinegar
1 cup hot water
½ cup fudge topping
½ cup chocolate chips, melted

Preheat over to 350 degrees. Grease bottom of two 9-inch round cake pans. Fit a circle of parchment paper large enough to cover one inch up the side of each cake pan. Heat the butter, brown sugar and sweetened condensed milk in a 2-quart saucepan over medium heat until the butter melts and brown sugar is dissolved. Do not boil. Pour half the brown sugar mixture into each pan. Sprinkle pecans over sugar mixture using ¾ cup pecans; set aside to cool. Combine the flour, granulated sugar, baking powder, baking soda, and salt together in a large bowl. Add the eggs, sour cream, oil, vanilla, vinegar and hot water; mix with a wooden spoon until the batter is smooth. Pour the batter in the cake pans – over the sugar mixture – and bake until a toothpick inserted into the cake center comes out clean, 35 to 40 minutes. Cool cakes in the pans for 10 minutes. Run a knife around the edge of the pans and turn cakes out onto a cooling rack. Remove the paper and cool completely. To assemble the cake, place one layer on a serving place, brown sugar side up. Spread the fudge topping over the brown sugar mixture. Place the second layer over the first layer, brown sugar side up, and drizzle with the melted chocolate chips. Sprinkle top with remaining ¼ cup of pecans. Frost the cake sides with your favorite chocolate icing.

Vickie Abrams
Berlin, Georgia

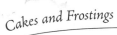
Cakes and Frostings

WHITE TEXAS SHEET CAKE

1 cup butter or margarine
1 cup water
2 cups self-rising flour
2 cups sugar
2 eggs, beaten
1 teaspoon almond extract
½ cup sour cream

In a large saucepan, bring butter and water to a boil. Remove from heat. Put flour and sugar in a large bowl; add butter and water mixture. Stir and then add eggs, sour cream and almond extract. Mix well and pour into a greased 15x-10-1-inch baking pan. Bake at 375 degrees for 20-22 minutes. Cool 20 minutes then spread frosting on top.

Frosting:
½ cup butter or margarine
¼ cup milk
1 (1 pound) box powdered sugar, sifted
½ teaspoon almond extract

Combine milk and margarine in a saucepan. Bring to a boil. Remove from heat; add powdered sugar and extract. Mix well. Spread over warm cake. Cut into small squares for party food, large sizes for dessert. Can get 80 small squares. This gets better as it ages.

Lemon Variation: Use lemon extract instead of almond. I use 2 tablespoons of lemon zest in the cake batter and about that much in the icing. Tastes just like lemon squares.

Chocolate Variation: Add ¼ cup cocoa to the cake mixture and 3 tablespoons to the frosting.

Jane Gibbs
Moultrie, Georgia

Cakes and Frostings

HOT MILK CAKE

½   cup (1 stick) butter
1   cup milk
2   cups sugar
4   eggs
2   cups all-purpose flour
1   tablespoon baking powder
1 ½ teaspoon vanilla extract
½   cup (1 stick) butter
Cinnamon and sugar to sprinkle

Heat 1 stick of butter and milk. Cream sugar and eggs. Add hot mixture, then add flour and baking powder and vanilla. Pour into 9x13-inch cake pan. Bake 35-40 minutes at 350 degrees. Spread one stick of butter over cake until the butter melted. Sprinkle with cinnamon and sugar.

Tonya Loraine Bustle
Coolidge, Georgia

GERMAN CHOCOLATE CHEWY CAKE
(A first edition favorite)

1   box German Chocolate cake mix
Eggs and oil according to cake mix directions
½   cup (1 stick) butter, softened
1   (8-ounce) package cream cheese, softened
1   (1 pound) box confectioner's sugar
1   cup coconut
1   cup pecans

Mix the German Chocolate cake mix as directed on package. Then add butter, cream cheese and powdered sugar into the cake batter. Sprinkle the coconut and pecans in a large baking dish; then pour the cake mixture on top of the coconut and pecans. Bake at 350 degrees for 35 to 45 minutes. Let cool and cut into squares. Yield: 15 to 20 depending on how big you cut the squares

Beth Kirkland
Nicholls, Georgia

Cakes and Frostings

CHOCOLATE COCA-COLA CAKE

(A first edition favorite)

2	cups all-purpose flour
2	cups sugar
1	cup (2 sticks) margarine
1	teaspoon baking soda
1	teaspoon vanilla extract
2	eggs
½	cup buttermilk
1	cup Coca-cola
2	tablespoons cocoa
2	cups miniature marshmallows

Put all dry ingredients into a large mixing bowl. In a saucepan, put margarine, cocoa, and Coca-cola. Bring to a boil. Pour over dry ingredients and mix thoroughly. Add eggs, vanilla, buttermilk and marshmallows; mix well. Pour into greased 9x13-inch sheet cake pan. Bake at 350 degrees for 40 to 45 minutes. When cake is done, ice while it is still hot.

Icing:

2	tablespoons (heaping) cocoa
½	cup (1 stick) margarine
¼	cup Coca-cola
1	pound box powdered sugar, sifted
1	cup chopped pecans
1	teaspoon vanilla extract

Bring Coca-cola, cocoa and margarine to a boil. Remove from heat. Add vanilla and sugar; mix well. Pour over cake. Work fast as the icing hardens quickly. If it hardens too quickly to spread, add some Coke. Nuts can be stirred into the icing or sprinkled on top.

A recipe from my days as a Home Economics teacher at Colquitt County High School. Can be made in two square pans—one for now and freeze one for later. Always a hit with children, teenagers and chocolate lovers of all ages.

Nancy Coleman
Hartsfield, Georgi

Cakes and Frostings

HONEY BUN CAKE

1	box super moist yellow cake mix
2/3	cup vegetable oil
4	eggs
1	(8-ounce) carton sour cream
1	cup packed brown sugar
1/3	cup chopped pecans
2	teaspoons ground cinnamon

Preheat oven to 350 degrees for shiny metal or glass pan (325 degrees for dark or non-stick pans). Spray bottom only of 13x9-inch pan with cooking spray; dust with flour. In large bowl, beat cake mix, oil, eggs and sour cream with electric mixer on low speed 30 seconds; beat on medium speed 2 minutes, scraping bowl occasionally. Spread half the batter in pan. In small bowl, stir together brown sugar, pecans and cinnamon; sprinkle over batter in pan. Carefully spread remaining batter evenly over pecan mixture. Bake 44-48 minutes or until deep golden brown. Remove from oven.

Icing:

1	cup powdered sugar
1	tablespoon milk
1	teaspoon vanilla extract

In a small bowl, stir icing ingredients until thin enough to spread. Prick surface of warm cake several times with fork. Spread icing over cake. Cool completely, about 1 hour. Store covered at room temperature.

Adrienne Hart
Berlin, Georgia

LEMON BLOSSOMS

1	box yellow cake mix
1	(3.5 ounce) box instant lemon pudding mix
4	large eggs
¾	cup vegetable oil

Preheat over to 350 degrees. Spray miniature muffin tins with cooking spray. Combine the cake mix, pudding mix, eggs and oil; blend well with electric mixer until smooth, about 2 minutes. Pour a small amount of batter into muffin tins, filling each muffin tin half full. Bake for 12 minutes. Turn out onto a tea towel.

Glaze:

4	cups powdered sugar
⅓	cup fresh lemon juice
1	lemon, zested
3	tablespoons vegetable oil
3	tablespoons water

Sift the sugar into a mixing bowl. Add the lemon juice, zest, oil and 3 tablespoons water. Mix with a spoon until smooth. With fingers, dip the cupcakes into the glaze while they're still warm, covering as much as the cake as possible or spoon the glaze over the warm cupcakes, turning them to completely coat. Place on wire racks with wax paper underneath to catch any drips. Let the glaze set thoroughly, about 1 hour, before storing in containers with tight-fitting lids.

I use these cupcakes a lot at brunch affairs. Very tasty!

Jane Gibbs
Moultrie, Georgia

Cakes and Frostings

BUTTER CREAM ICING

½   cup white shortening
½   cup butter or margarine
1   teaspoon vanilla extract
1   (1 pound) box powdered sugar, sifted
2   tablespoons milk (more if needed)

Cream shortening and margarine. Add vanilla. Gradually mix in sugar. Add milk as necessary to achieve desired spreading consistency. **Note:** To make a ivory-colored frosting, omit the shortening and use 1 cup butter or margarine.

Variation: You can change the flavor by substituting most any juice for the milk. For example, Key lime juice, orange juice, lemon juice, or strawberry juice.

Nancy Coleman
Hartsfield, Georgia

CARAMEL ICING

1 ½   cups light brown sugar
½   cup dark brown sugar
1   tablespoon shortening
1   tablespoon light corn syrup
½   cup milk

Mix all ingredients together and bring to a boil, stirring often. Cook to soft ball stage, 240 degrees on a candy thermometer.

In mixing bowl with electric mixer, mix together:

⅓   cup shortening
¼   cup milk
2 ½   cups sifted powdered sugar
1   teaspoon vanilla extract

Pour hot brown sugar mixture over powdered sugar mixture. Beat two minutes until smooth and of consistency to spread on cake.

This is a very creamy frosting and doesn't get too hard like some caramel frostings do.

Nancy Coleman
Hartsfield, Georgia

LEMON CREAM CHEESE ICING

6   ounces cream cheese, at room temperature
¼   cup softened butter or margarine
4 ½   cups powdered sugar, sifted
1   teaspoon grated lemon peel
½   teaspoon lemon extract

Combine cream cheese and butter in mixing bowl. Blend thoroughly with an electric mixer. Gradually beat in powdered sugar. Add lemon peel and extract. Beat until smooth and creamy. Spread on cake.

Virginia Hart
Moultrie, Georgia

PERFECTLY CHOCOLATE FROSTING

½   cup (1 stick) margarine
⅔   cup Hershey's cocoa
1   teaspoon vanilla extract
3   cups powdered sugar, sifted
⅓   cup milk

Melt butter. Stir in cocoa. Add powdered sugar and milk alternately, beating on medium speed. Stir in vanilla. Frost cake.

Sheila Brown
Moultrie, Georgia

Candies

COTTON AND THE WAR

The Civil War severely impaired cotton production in Georgia. Many of the textile mills were located in the North. During the war, New England mills shut down due to the halted cotton supply. Much of the state's cotton was exported to England. Some Southerners thought that England would join their side in order to keep English textile mills running. Such was not the case.

Georgia planters burned cotton warehouses rather than let them fall into enemy hands. In 1862 a resolution was passed in the Confederate Congress restricting cotton production. Some farmers protested and planted anyway. However, the result in 1862 was a 60,000 bale crop rather than the usual 700,000 average. The war also caused Georgians to divert acreage to provide the needs of the Confederate army.

After the war, sharecroppers were used to farm the plantations. There was a strong demand for cotton once the war ended and those seeking to borrow money found that cotton was worth more as collateral than the land.

INDEX

PINE BARK

1   cup (2 sticks) butter
1   cup brown sugar
2   (12-ounce) bags milk chocolate chips
1 ½ sleeves saltine crackers
2   (1- ounce) squares white chocolate candy coating

Line shallow baking sheet with foil; coat with cooking spray. Place crackers on baking sheet, salted side up. Melt butter in sauce pan; add brown sugar and cook until caramelized, about 3 minutes. Pour mixture over crackers and spread evenly. Bake in 350 degree oven for 8 minutes. Remove from oven and sprinkle chocolate chips on top. Spread chocolate as it melts. Microwave white chocolate on 50% power for 2 minutes, stirring every 30 seconds. Cool slightly. Spoon white chocolate into a pint ziptop freezer bag. Squeeze all the air out and seal. Snip off a very small corner of the bag and squeeze coating from bag drizzling white chocolate over milk chocolate. Refrigerate 2 hours. Break apart.

Festive gift idea when presented in a cellophane bag tied with a bow.

Nancy Coleman
Hartsfield, Georgia

COCONUT BALLS

½   cup (1 stick) butter, melted
2   (1-pound) boxes powdered sugar
2   (7-ounce) packages coconut
1   tablespoon vanilla extract
1   (14-ounce) can sweetened condensed milk
1   (8-ounce) box semisweet chocolate
½   block paraffin wax

Combine the butter, sugar, coconut, vanilla and milk; mix well. Shape into balls. Chill for one hour. Melt the chocolate and paraffin in top of double boiler over hot water. Dip balls in chocolate mixture, then place on wax paper to harden.

Sheila Brown
Moultrie, Georgia

DIVINITY

2½ cups sugar
½   cup light corn syrup
½   cup water
1   cup chopped nuts
¼   teaspoon salt
2   egg whites
1   teaspoon vanilla extract

Combine sugar, water and corn syrup in a 3-quart saucepan; cook over low heat. Cook to hard ball stage (260 degrees on a candy thermometer). Remove from heat. Beat egg whites in a large bowl until stiff peaks form. Pour hot sugar mixture in a very thin stream over egg white while beating constantly. Add vanilla and continue beating until mixture holds its shape. Stir in pecans. Drop by teaspoonfuls onto wax paper.

Sheila Brown
Moultrie, Georgia

FANTASY DIVINITY

½   cup water
2   cups sugar
1   (7-ounce) jar marshmallow crème
½   teaspoon vanilla extract (use clear extract for pure white divinity)
1   cup chopped pecans (optional)

In a large heavy saucepan, stir together the water and sugar. Bring to a boil and cook until the mixtures reaches 260 degrees on a candy thermometer. Mix with marshmallow créme, vanilla and nuts. Stir by hand until stiff. Spoon onto wax paper.

Variation: Use ½ cup crushed peppermint candies instead of the nuts.

Nancy Coleman
Hartsfield, Georgia

Candies

CHRISTMAS FUDGE

3   cups sugar
¾   cup margarine
⅔   cup evaporated milk
1   (12-ounce) package semi-sweet chocolate chips
1   (7-ounce) jar marshmallow crème
1   cup chopped pecans
1   teaspoon vanilla extract

Place margarine in large microwave-safe bowl. Microwave on high for 1 minute or until melted. Add sugar and milk; mix well. Microwave at full power for 3 minutes, stir, and cook an additional 2 minutes or until mixture begins to boil. Mix well scraping sides of bowl. Microwave 5 1/2 minutes, stirring after 3 minutes. Gradually stir in chocolate and marshmallow crème until completely melted. Add pecans and vanilla. Pour into a greased 9x13-inch pan. Cool at room temperature; cut into squares. Yield: about 3 pounds.

This is not my original recipe, but even I can make this fudge without failure.

Thomas Coleman
Hartsfield, Georgia

FUDGE

Chocolate Fudge

5	ounces evaporated milk
4	tablespoons butter
2	cups sugar
½	cup chopped pecans
¼	teaspoon salt
1	(7-ounce) jar marshmallow crème
6	ounces semisweet chocolate chips
1 ½	teaspoons vanilla extract

Pour milk, butter, sugar and salt in saucepan. Cook on medium heat until it reaches 230 degrees on a candy thermometer. Stir in chocolate chips, vanilla, marshmallow crème and nuts. Pour into greased 9x13-inch pan.

White Fudge

5	ounces evaporated milk
4	tablespoons butter
2	cups sugar
¼	teaspoon salt
1 ½	teaspoons vanilla extract
6	ounces white chocolate chips
½	large bag marshmallows
½	cup chopped pecans

Combine sugar, butter, salt and milk. Cook on medium heat until it reached 230 degrees on a candy thermometer. Stir in other ingredients and mix well. Pour on top of chocolate fudge or mix it all together and swirl it. Cool. Cut into squares.

Sheila Brown
Moultrie, Georgia

PEANUT BUTTER FUDGE

(A first edition favorite)

1	(12-ounce) jar creamy peanut butter
1	(7 ½ -ounce) jar marshmallow crème
1	teaspoon vanilla extract
1	cup chopped salted peanuts
2	cups sugar
2	cups firmly packed light brown sugar
¾	cup milk
½	teaspoon salt
¼	cup salted peanut halves

Combine peanut butter, marshmallow crème, vanilla and chopped peanuts in a large bowl; set aside. Combine sugar, milk, and salt; stir well. Cook over medium heat until mixture comes to a boil; boil 4 minutes, stirring occasionally. Remove from heat and pour over peanut butter mixture; stir quickly until well blended. Pour into a buttered 13x9x2-inch pan and sprinkle with peanut halves. Allow candy to cool for at least 2 hours. Cut fudge into squares. Yield: 3 ½ dozen.

Gail Thompson
Moultrie, Georgia

Appearing on everything from clothing hang-tags and towels to shirts and pants, Cotton Incorporated's Seal of Cotton trademark is the central visual and driving force behind cotton's continued popularity with consumers. Introduced in 1973, today more than eight out of ten consumers can identify it. It is one of America's most visible and well-respected trademarks.

SOFT AND CHEWY CARAMELS

1   cup butter
1   (16-ounce) box light brown sugar
1   (14-ounce) can sweetened condensed milk
1   cup light corn syrup
Vegetable cooking spray

Line an 8-inch square baking pan with foil, extending foil over edges of pan. Generously coat foil with cooking spray and set aside. Melt 1 cup butter in 3-quart saucepan over low heat. Stir in brown sugar, condensed milk, and corn syrup until smooth. Bring mixture to a boil. Cook over medium heat, stirring often, until a candy thermometer registers 235 degrees. Remove mixture from heat and stir by hand 1 minute or until mixture is smooth and no longer bubbling. Quickly pour mixture into prepared pan and let stand 3 hours or until cool. Lift foil and caramel out of pan. Cut caramels into 1-inch pieces with a buttered knife. (You can wrap each piece with plastic wrap) Makes 64 pieces

These are softer than store-bought caramels.

Charlotte Mathis
Moultrie, Georgia

SOUTHERN PECAN PRALINES
(A first edition favorite)

3   cups packed brown sugar   ¼   teaspoon butter or margarine
1   cup whipping cream   2   cups chopped pecans
2   tablespoons corn syrup   1¼   teaspoons vanilla extract
¼   teaspoon salt

In a large heavy saucepan over medium heat, bring brown sugar, cream, corn syrup, and salt to a boil, stirring constantly. Cook until a candy thermometer reads 234 degrees (soft ball stage). Remove from heat. Add butter. Do not stir. Cool until candy thermometer reads 150 degrees (about 35 minutes). Stir in pecans and vanilla. Stir with a wooden spoon until candy just begins to thicken, but is still glossy, about 5-7 minutes. Quickly drop by heaping teaspoonfuls onto waxed paper, spread to form 2-inch patties. Store in airtight container. Yield: 3-4 dozen.

Lynn Tillman
Quitman, Georgia

PRETZEL TURTLES

1 bag mini twisted pretzels
1 (12-ounce) bag Rolos
Toasted pecan halves

Preheat oven 250 degrees. Line cookie sheet with foil. Coat foil with cooking spray. Cover cookie sheet with mini twisted pretzels. Place one Rolo in center of each pretzel. Heat for 5 minutes. Remove from oven and press toasted pecan halves into center of Rolos. Chill.

Brenda Morris
Ocilla, Georgia

DIXIE PEANUT BRITTLE

2 cups granulated sugar
1 cup light corn syrup
½ cup water
½ teaspoon salt
3 cups raw peanuts, skins on
2 tablespoons butter
2 teaspoons baking soda

In a heavy saucepan, heat sugar, syrup, water and salt to a rolling boil. Add peanuts. Reduce heat to medium and stir constantly. Cook until syrup spins a thread (293 degrees). Add butter, then baking soda. Beat rapidly and pour on a buttered surface spreading to ¼ inch thickness. When cool, break into pieces.

Brenda Morris
Ocilla, Georgia

PEANUT BRITTLE

1 ½ cups sugar
1-inch square paraffin wax
½ cup light corn syrup
1 teaspoon soda
1 ½ cups raw peanuts

Cook sugar, paraffin, syrup, and peanuts until brown, about 15 minutes. Then add soda and stir 1 minute. Drop onto wax paper and let cool.

Mary Barber
Tifton, Georgia

TRASH

1 pound white chocolate
3 cups Corn Chex and 3 cups Rice Chex
3 cups Cheerios
2 cups pretzel sticks
2 cups dry roasted peanuts
1 (12-ounce) package M & M's

Slowly melt white chocolate in microwave. Combine Corn Chex, Rice Chex, Cheerios, pretzel sticks, peanuts, and M&M's in large bowl. Pour chocolate over mixture and coat evenly. Spread on wax paper and cool. Break into pieces. Store in air tight container.

You may substitute 6 cups Crispix for the Corn Chex and Rice Chex.

Brenda Morris
Ocilla, Georgia

PEANUT BUTTER CANDY

1½ pounds white chocolate
1   cup peanut butter
2   cups dry roasted peanuts
3   cups miniature marshmallows
3   cups Rice Krispies

Melt chocolate. Mix in peanut butter, dry roasted peanuts, marshmallows and Rice Krispies. Mix well, use teaspoon to dip out and place on wax paper to cool.

Shirley Tankersley
Ocilla, Georgia

TIC TAC TOES

2   (6-ounce) packages butterscotch or semi-sweet chocolate chips
1   (3-ounce) can chow mien noodles
1   (7-ounce) can salted peanuts

Melt chips in double boiler over hot water. Add other ingredients and stir until well blended. Drop by teaspoons onto wax paper.

Nancy Coleman
Hartsfield, Georgia

CARAMEL CORN

2   (4-ounce) bags of puffed corn
½   cup (1 stick) margarine
1   cup light brown sugar
½   cup light corn syrup
½   teaspoon baking soda
½   teaspoon vanilla extract

In a large saucepan, bring margarine, brown sugar and corn syrup to boiling point; add baking soda and vanilla. Boil for four minutes, stirring often. Place puffed corn in a large pan. Pour hot mixture over puffed corn and mix well. Spread corn in large pan or cookie sheet. Bake at 225 degrees for one hour. Stir from the bottom of the pan every 15 minutes. Take it up in another large pan and cool. Place in airtight containers. (I sometimes add nuts, pecans or mixed.)

We make this for all of our friends to munch on when we're at the beach or tailgating in Athens at the University of Georgia football games.

Jane Gibbs
Moultrie, Georgia

SUGARED PEANUTS

1   cup granulated sugar
½   cup water
2   cups raw shelled peanuts (with skins on)

Dissolve sugar in water in saucepan over medium heat. Add peanuts and continue to cook over medium heat, stirring frequently. Cook until peanuts are completely sugared coated and no syrup is left. Pour onto ungreased cookie sheet, spreading so that peanuts are separated as much as possible. Bake at 300 degrees for approximately 30 minutes, stirring at five minute intervals. Cool completely before storing.

Brenda Morris
Ocilla, Georgia

Cookies

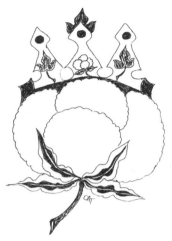

THE KING RETURNS

When the Civil War ended in 1865, the scramble was on to find the funds for seed, livestock, labor and equipment to begin production again. Within fifteen years, the state reached its first million-bale harvest.

And, for the second time in history, cotton fabric became America's favorite. Part of cotton's comeback popularity can be attributed to the demand for denim jeans or "levis," which were created just prior to the war by a man named Levi Strauss. He produced these work-hardy pants for the miners during the 1849-1860 California Gold Rush.

After the turn of the century, steamships were the primary source of transportation for cotton. The valuable cargo even took precedence over passengers who were forced to sit in darkness behind walls of cotton bales.

Because it took one hour to gin each bale of cotton, large lines of cotton wagons were common sites at gin yards. In the 1920's, yields were high and the going rate was a dollar a pound.

During the Great Depression, the success of communities in the Cotton Belt teetered on each season's harvest. Economic prosperity was measured in cotton sacks. In the 1930's, school dismissed and entire families pitched in to help bring in the crop.

INDEX

FUDGY BROWNIES
(A first edition favorite)

4   (1-ounce) squares unsweetened chocolate
⅔   cup butter or shortening
1 ⅓ cups all-purpose flour
½   teaspoon salt
1   teaspoon baking powder
4   eggs
2   cups sugar
2   teaspoons vanilla extract
1   cup chopped nuts

Melt chocolate with butter in saucepan over very low heat stirring constantly until smooth OR microwave at 50 percent power for 2 minutes. Cool slightly. Beat eggs thoroughly and gradually blend in sugar. Blend in chocolate mixture and vanilla. Add dry ingredients and mix well; stir in nuts. Spread in greased 13 X 9-inch pan. Bake at 350 degrees for 25 minutes for moist chewy brownies or about 30 minutes for cake-like brownies. Cool in pan and cut into squares or bars. Yield: About 24.

Mississippi Mud Variation: While brownies are cooking, melt 1 stick butter and ⅓ cup cocoa in saucepan over low heat. Add 1 box sifted confectioner's sugar, 1 teaspoon vanilla extract and about ¾ cup milk stirring with wire whisk until smooth. When brownies are done, remove from oven and top with one small bag miniature marshmallows. Pour frosting over marshmallows.

I started making this recipe when I was in high school. It earned me the title of "brownie queen." "Mud" is a popular treat for family fish fries, cookouts and reunions. Children, and quite a few adults, love them.

Nancy Coleman
Hartsfield, Georgia

QUICK BROWNIES

(A first edition favorite)

1	stick butter
2	squares unsweetened chocolate
1	cup sugar
2	eggs
½	teaspoon vanilla
¼	cup all-purpose flour
¼	teaspoon salt
1	cup chopped walnuts (optional)

Melt together butter and chocolate; take saucepan off the heat. Stir in sugar; add eggs and vanilla. Mix well. Stir in flour and salt. Add walnuts (optional). Bake brownies in a buttered and floured 8-inch square pan at 325 degrees for 35-40 minutes.

You can cut these brownies into squares, once they have cooled, and eat them out of the pan, but it is so much nicer to pile them on a fancy plate, from which people are going to eat them with their hands, anyway. If you want to smarten up your act, you can put a square of brownie on a plate with a little blob of whipped cream and a scattering of shaved chocolate.

Connie Mobley
Moultrie, Georgia

BROWNIES FILLED WITH CARAMEL

1	package brownie mix
1	cup coarsely chopped walnuts, toasted
½	pound milk chocolate-covered caramel patties

Prepare brownie mix according to package directions, adding walnuts. Spoon half of mixture into a greased 13x9-inch baking pan. Place caramel patties in an even layer over the mixture. Spoon remaining batter over candies. Bake at 350 degrees for 30-35 minutes or until done.

Teresa Walker
Tifton, Georgia

BLOND BROWNIES

½	cup shortening	1	teaspoon vanilla extract
½	teaspoon baking powder	1	egg
1	tablespoon milk	½	cup chopped walnuts
⅛	teaspoon salt	1	cup all-purpose flour
1	cup firmly packed brown sugar		

Heat oven to 350 degrees. Grease 8-inch square pan. Combine shortening and milk in large microwavable safe bowl. Microwave at 50% (medium). Stir after one minute. Repeat until melted. Stir in brown sugar. Add egg. Stir until blended. Combine flour, baking powder, and salt. Stir in vanilla and nuts. Spread in pan. Bake for 27-30 minutes or until toothpick comes out clean. Yield: 12 servings

Teresa Walker
Tifton, Georgia

OOEY-GOOEY PEANUT BUTTER CHOCOLATE BROWNIES

¾ cut fat-free sweetened condensed milk, divided
¼ cup butter or margarine, melted and cooled
¼ cup fat-free milk
1 (18.25 ounce) package devil's food cake mix
1 large egg white, lightly beaten
1 (7-ounce) jar marshmallow crème
½ cup peanut butter chips

Preheat oven to 350 degrees. Combine ¼ cup condensed milk, butter, milk, cake mix and egg white (batter will be stiff). Coat bottom of 13x9-inch pan with cooking spray. Press two-thirds of the batter into prepared pan. Flour hands; use hands to press mixture evenly over bottom of pan. It will be a thin layer. Bake at 350 degrees for 10 minutes. Remove from oven. Combine ½ cup condensed milk and marshmallow crème in a bowl; stir in peanut butter chips. Spread marshmallow mixture evenly over cooked brownie layer. Carefully drop remaining cake batter by spoonfuls over marshmallow mixture. Return to oven and bake at 350 degrees for 30 minutes. Cool completely in pan on wire rack. Yield: 2 dozen brownies.

Nancy Coleman
Hartsfield, Georgia

Cookies

CHEW BREAD

½   butter, softened
1   box (2 cups packed) light brown sugar
2   eggs
2   cups self-rising flour
1   teaspoon vanilla
1   cup chopped pecans

In a large mixing bowl, combine butter and brown sugar; add eggs and beat well. Blend in remaining ingredients. Pour into 9x13-inch baking pan. Bake at 300 degrees for 35-45 minutes until set.

Cassandra Bullington
Cordele, Georgia

PECAN CHEWIES

½   cup butter, softened
1   (16-ounce) box brown sugar
1   teaspoon vanilla extract
3   eggs
1 ½   cups self-rising flour
1   cup chopped pecans

Heat oven to 350 degrees. Grease 13x9-inch pan. Beat butter, brown sugar, and vanilla in large bowl on medium speed until light and fluffy. Add eggs, one at a time, beating well after each addition. Stir in flour and pecans. Pour into pan. Bake 30-35 minutes until golden brown. Cool completely. Cut into bars. Yield: 48 bars.

Teresa Walker
Tifton, Georgia

SALTED PEANUT CHEWS

1½   cups all-purpose flour
½   teaspoon baking powder
¼   teaspoon soda
½   teaspoon salt
⅔   cup light brown sugar
½   cup soft butter
2   egg yolks
1   teaspoon vanilla extract
3   cups mini marshmallows
1   package peanut butter morsels
⅔   cup light corn syrup
¼   cup butter
2   teaspoons vanilla extract
2   cups Rice Krispies
2   cups salted peanuts
Milk chocolate morsels, optional

Combine flour, baking powder, soda, salt, brown sugar, butter, egg yolks, and vanilla in large bowl. Press into 9x13-inch dish. Bake 350 degrees 12 to 15 minutes. Sprinkle marshmallows over crust and bake 1-2 minutes. Combine peanut butter morsels, corn syrup, butter and vanilla in saucepan and cook until smooth. Remove from heat and stir in Rice Krispies and peanuts. Spread on top of marshmallows. If you would like, you can drizzle melted chocolate on top.

Brenda Morris
Ocilla, Georgia

Cutting brownies is much easier if you use a plastic knife. The brownies don't stick to the knife.

INCREDIBLE EDIBLES COOKIES

¾   cup butter, melted
2   cups crushed graham cracker crumbs
1   jar (12-ounce) peanut butter
2   cups powdered sugar
12   ounces semisweet chocolate morsels

In a medium bowl, combine melted butter, graham cracker crumbs, peanut butter, and sugar; beat with wooden spoon or electric beater until thoroughly mixed and crumbly. Press evenly into ungreased 9x13 inch pan and set aside. In top of double boiler, melt chocolate over hot (not boiling) water until smooth; spread evenly over peanut butter mixture in pan. Let stand at room temperature until chocolate hardens. When hard, cut into small squares (the cookies are very rich). Yield: about 3 ½ dozen cookies

Mary Walker
Tifton, Georgia

PUMPKIN BARS

1   box pound cake mix
1   egg, beaten
2   tablespoons butter
1   cup chopped, salted roasted peanuts
4   teaspoon pumpkin spice
½   teaspoon salt
2   eggs beaten
1   (16-ounce) can pumpkin
1   (8- ounce) package cream cheese
1   (14-ounce) can sweetened condensed milk

Mix cake mix, egg, butter, chopped peanuts and pumpkin spice together and press into thin cookie sheet. Mix salt, 2 beaten eggs, pumpkin, cream cheese and sweetened condensed milk and pour on top of first mixture. Bake at 350 degrees for 25 minutes. Cool and cut.

Ottis Walker
Tifton, Georgia

LEMON COCONUT SQUARES

(A first edition favorite)

Crust:

1½	cups all-purpose flour
½	cup brown sugar
½	cup (1 stick) butter, melted

Grease 9x13-inch pan well. Spread mixture over bottom. Bake at 275 degrees for 10-15 minutes.

Filling:

2	eggs
1	cup brown sugar
½	cup coconut
1	cup chopped nuts
2	tablespoons flour
½	teaspoon baking powder
¼	teaspoon salt
½	teaspoon vanilla

Chop coconut in food processor or blender so it will not be stringy. Mix all ingredients well, beating 2 to 3 minutes. Spread over baked bottom layer. Bake 20 minutes at 350 degrees or until brown.

Topping:

6	tablespoon lemon juice
	Powdered sugar

Mix until thick enough to spread on top of filling. Cool; cut into squares.

Susan York
Pavo, Georgia

SHORTBREAD LEMON BARS

1½   cups all purpose flour
½   cup confectioner's sugar
¾   cup cold margarine

Filling

4   eggs
2   cups sugar
⅔   cup lemon juice
¼   cup all-purpose flour
1   teaspoon baking powder

Topping

2   cups (16-ounces) sour cream
⅓   cup sugar
½   teaspoon vanilla extract

In a food processor, combine flour, confectioner's sugar. Cut in butter until crumbly; process until mixture forms a ball. Pat into a greased 13x9-inch baking pan. Bake at 350 degrees for 12-14 minutes or until set and the edges are lightly browned. Meanwhile, in a mixing bowl, combine the filling ingredients; mix well. Pour over hot crust. Bake for 14-16 minutes or until set and lightly browned. Meanwhile, in a bowl, combine topping ingredients. Spread over filling. Bake 7-9 minutes longer or until topping is set. Cool on a wire rack. Refrigerate overnight. Cut into bars before serving.

Cindy Tyus
Moultrie, Georgia

RICH BROWNIE CUPCAKES

¾   cup margarine
2   squares semisweet chocolate
1   square unsweetened chocolate
1 ¾ cups sugar
4   eggs
1   teaspoon vanilla extract
1   cup all-purpose flour
2   tablespoons cocoa
⅛   teaspoon salt
1   cup chopped pecans

Melt butter and chocolate squares in microwave. Stir in sugar. Add eggs, one at a time, stirring well after each addition; stir in vanilla. Combine flour, cocoa, and salt; add to chocolate mixture, stirring until smooth. Stir in pecans. Spoon batter into miniature muffin tins that have been greased with cooking spray, filling three-fourths full. Bake at 350 degrees for 10-12 minutes. (Time will vary with ovens. Watch closely and remove when toothpick comes out clean. They are easy to over cook)

Charlotte Mathis
Moultrie, Georgia

Less than 3.5 million people in America live on the farm today compared to 29.8 million in 1900. That averages out to be less than 2 percent of the U. S. population.

MACAROON COOKIES

½   cup margarine, softened
1   (3-ounce) package cream cheese, softened
¾   cup sugar
1   egg yolk
1   teaspoon almond extract
1¼   cups all-purpose flour
2   teaspoons baking powder
¼   teaspoon salt
5   cups sweetened flaked coconut, divided
1   (10-ounce) package Hershey's Kisses, unwrapped

Beat margarine, cream cheese, and sugar with electric mixer until blended. Add egg yolks and almond extract, beating until mixture is blended. Combine flour, baking powder, and salt; gradually add to butter mixture, beating until blended. Stir in 3 cups coconut. Cover and chill 1 hour. Shape dough into 1-inch balls; roll balls in remaining 2 cups coconut, and place on ungreased baking sheets. Bake at 350 degrees for 11-13 minutes or until cookies are lightly browned. Remove from oven and press 1 chocolate kiss into center of each warm cookie. Cool on baking sheet for 1 minute and remove to wire rack to cool completely.
Yield: 4 dozen

Charlotte Mathis
Moultrie, Georgia

SIMPLE PEANUT BUTTER COOKIES

1   cup creamy peanut butter
1   cup sugar
1   egg
1   teaspoon vanilla

Cream peanut butter and sugar in mixing bowl. Add egg and vanilla. Shape into small balls. Place on cookie sheet and flatten with a fork. Bake at 350 degrees for 8 -10 minutes.

Cassandra Bullington
Cordele, Georgia

Cookies

PEANUT BUTTER COOKIES

1	cup peanut butter
½	cup sugar
1	egg
4	tablespoons semi-sweet chocolate, melted
½	cup finely chopped peanuts

Preheat oven to 325 degrees. Mix peanut butter, sugar and egg until well blended. Refrigerate for 30 minutes. Remove and roll mixture into 18 balls. Place on ungreased cookie sheet 2 inches apart. Flatten each ball by using a fork to make a criss-cross pattern. Bake 18-20 minutes or until lightly browned. Cool for 5 minutes on cookie sheet and then cool completely on a wire rack. Melt chocolate. Dip one end of cookie into melted chocolate and then dip into chopped peanuts. Repeat with other side of cookie. Place on cookie sheet lined with wax paper and refrigerate until chocolate hardens.

Brenda Morris
Ocilla, Georgia

ANGEL COOKIES

1	cup shortening
½	cup granulated sugar
½	cup brown sugar
1	egg
1	teaspoon vanilla extract
2	cups all-purpose flour
1	teaspoon soda
1	teaspoon cream of tartar

Preheat oven to 375 degrees. Cream shortening and sugar until light and fluffy. Add egg and vanilla; beat well. Combine flour, soda and cream of tartar; add to creamed mixture. Roll into small balls about the size of walnuts. Dip top in water and roll in sugar. Place sugar side up on greased cookie sheet. Bake for 10 to 12 minutes. Yield: 4 dozen large cookies.

Cookies are my specialty. Every year I bake several recipes and give a variety to my friends. I always have a few regulars, but I always try to add a new one. Angel Cookies are great for Christmas because of their name. The water and sugar make a white glaze. You can also use colored sugar, but I like the white sugar better.

Nancy Coleman
Hartsfield, Georgia

The cotton gin was invented by Eli Whitney in 1793 while he was visiting a plantation outside Savannah, Georgia. Its comb-like mechanism which removes the seed from the lint replaced the labor of 50 workers.

OATMEAL COOKIES

1	cup butter-flavored shortening or margarine
1	cup brown sugar
1	cup granulated sugar
2	cups all-purpose flour
3	eggs
2	tablespoons milk
1	teaspoon vanilla extract
½	teaspoon salt
1	teaspoon baking soda
2	cups oatmeal
1	cup coconut
1	cup chopped nuts
12	ounces semi-sweet chocolate chips

Preheat oven to 350 degrees. Cream shortening; gradually add brown sugar and granulated sugar until light and fluffy. (This step is the key to the success of this recipe. The lighter and fluffier, the better.) Add eggs and mix well; add vanilla and milk. Gradually stir in flour, salt and baking soda. With a wooden spoon, stir in oatmeal, coconut, pecans, and chocolate chips. This mixture will become very stiff. Drop by rounded teaspoons onto ungreased cookie sheet. Bake for 10 minutes for a soft chewy cookie and 12 minutes for a crisp cookie. Remove from pan immediately and cool on wire racks. Store in air-tight container. Freezes well. Yield: about 5 dozen.

Variation: Substitute raisins for chocolate chips.

In our family, this is "the" cookie recipe.

Nancy Coleman
Hartsfield, Georgia

HAYSTACKS COOKIES

2	(9-ounce) bags butterscotch bits
1	(8-ounce) jar dry roasted peanuts
1	can chow mien noodles

Melt bits over water. Stir in peanuts and noodles. Drop onto wax paper.

Mary Walker
Tifton, Georgia

MOCHA NUT COOKIES
(A first edition favorite)

1   (12-ounce) package semi-sweet chocolate chips, divided
2   tablespoons instant coffee
2   teaspoons boiling water
1¼ cups all-purpose flour
¾   teaspoon baking soda
½   cup chopped nuts
½   teaspoon salt
½   cup butter, softened
½   cup sugar
½   cup firmly packed brown sugar
1   egg

Preheat oven to 350 degrees. Melt over hot (not boiling) water, ½ cup semi-sweet chocolate chips (or melt in microwave at 50 percent power for about 1 minute). Stir until smooth; cool to room temperature. In small cup, dissolve instant coffee in boiling water; set aside. In large bowl, combine butter, sugar, brown sugar and coffee; beat until creamy. Add egg and melted chocolate chips; mix well. Gradually add dry ingredients. Stir in remaining chocolate chips and nuts. Drop by rounded teaspoons onto greased cookie sheet. Bake for 10-12 minutes. Allow to stand briefly before removing from cookie sheets. Place on wire racks to cool completely. Yield: about 24 3-inch cookies.

A good recipe for chocolate lovers. The coffee intensifies the chocolate flavor. Excellent while still warm and chewy. Do not store with other cookies or all of the cookies will tastes like coffee.

Nancy Coleman
Hartsfield, Georgia

CRANBERRY TREASURE COOKIES

1 ⅔ cups all-purpose flour
1   teaspoon baking soda
½   teaspoon salt
½   cup butter or margarine, softened
¾   cup firmly packed brown sugar
1   egg
1   (10-ounce) package Toll House white baking pieces
1   cup dried cranberries
½   cup pecans, coarsely chopped
1   teaspoon grated orange rind

Preheat oven to 375 degrees. Grease two large cookie sheets. In a small bowl, combine flour, baking soda and salt and set aside. In a large mixer bowl, beat butter and brown sugar until creamy. Blend in egg. Gradually beat in flour mixture. Stir in white baking pieces, cranberries, pecans and orange rind. Drop by heaping measuring tablespoonfuls onto prepared cookie sheets. Bake 12 – 14 minutes until golden brown. Let stand 2 minutes and remove from cookie sheets. Store loosely covered up to 3 days. Yield: 2 dozen.

Margaret Anderson
Meigs, Georgia

The highest number of cotton acres planted in Georgia (since accurate records were kept) occurred in 1914 when 5.15 million acres were planted.

BUTTER PECAN COOKIES

(Crescent Cookies)

1   cup (2 sticks) butter
2   cups flour
2   cups chopped nuts
5   tablespoons sugar
2   tablespoons vanilla extract
1   teaspoon salt
1   tablespoon water
Powdered sugar

Cream butter; add sugar, vanilla and water. Sift flour and salt together and stir into mixture. Add pecans and mix thoroughly. Using portions about the size of a walnut; roll into desired shapes: fingers, balls, crescents, etc. Bake at 300 degrees until very light brown, 25 to 30 minutes. While warm, roll in powdered sugar.

These cookies are known by several names—crescents, pecan fingers, sand cookies. By whatever name, they are my favorite cookies. I hardly ever make them because I would eat the whole batch!

Lois Clark
Cairo, Georgia

CHERRY NUT COOKIES

1   box yellow cake mix
½   cup oil
1   egg
2   teaspoons water
1   (6 ounce) jar maraschino cherries, mashed or chopped
Chopped nuts, as many as you like

Combine all ingredients, including juice from cherries. Roll into balls and bake at 350 degrees until light brown. Remove from oven and cool on wire racks. Yield: 50 small cookies

Tonya Loraine Bustle
Coolidge, Georgia

RED VELVET COOKIES

1   box red velvet cake mix
2   eggs
½   cup oil

Mix all ingredients until smooth. Roll in 1-inch balls and place on lightly greased cookie sheet. Use the bottom of a glass to flatten slightly. Bake at 375 degrees for 8-10 minutes. Cool on rack. Frost with Cream Cheese Frosting. Yield: about 48 cookies.

Cream Cheese Frosting:
1   (8-ounce) package cream cheese
¼   cup (½ stick) butter
2   teaspoons milk
1   teaspoon vanilla extract
4   cups powdered sugar, sifted

Combine cream cheese, butter, milk and vanilla in a mixing bowl. Mix with electric mixer until creamy. Slowly add sugar. Frost cooled cookies.

These are especially pretty at Christmas or Valentine's Day.

Jane Gibbs
Moultrie, Georgia

Some recipes call for confectioners sugar while others call for powdered sugar. They are the same. In fact, the some companies label their product as "confectioners sugar;" some label it as "powdered sugar," while one uses "confectioners powdered sugar."

NUT CRISPS

(A first edition favorite)

2	eggs
2½	cups light brown sugar, firmly packed
1½	cups coarsely chopped nuts
½	teaspoon baking powder
¼	teaspoon salt
1	teaspoon vanilla extract
1¾	cups flour

Beat eggs until very light and foamy; then beat in brown sugar. Gradually add nuts, flour sifted with baking powder, and salt; stir in vanilla. Chill several hours. Cut off approximately one heaping teaspoonful and roll between hands into sticks about 2 inches long. Place about 3 inches apart on greased cookie sheet. Or, if you don't have time to chill it, drop by teaspoonfuls onto greased cookie sheet about 3 inches apart. Bake at 325 degrees 12 to 15 minutes. Remove from cookie sheet while warm. Cool completely on wire racks. Yield: about 5 dozen.

The brown sugar and nuts provide a caramel-like flavor. Takes a while to shape, but children can help.

Nancy Coleman
Hartsfield, Georgia

Brown sugar is white sugar to which molasses has been added to create a caramel-like flavor. It is much softer than white sugar and creates a most, chewy cookie or cake. Dark brown sugar has more molasses than light brown. To measure brown sugar, firmly pack into a measuring cup.

COWBOY COOKIES

5	cups sifted flour
2	teaspoons soda
1	teaspoon baking powder
¼	teaspoon salt
1	cup sugar
1	cup shortening
4	eggs
1	stick butter
2	cups oatmeal
2	cups brown sugar
1	(12-ounce) package semi-sweet chocolate chips
2	teaspoons vanilla extract

Sift together and set aside the flour, soda, salt, and baking powder. Blend together shortening and sugar. Add eggs and beat until light and fluffy. Add flour mixture and mix well. Add oats, vanilla, and chocolate. Dough is crumbly. Drop teaspoonfuls onto greased cookie sheet. Bake 15 minutes at 350 degrees.

Lindsey Walker Kaiser
Tifton, Georgia

Sometimes called "white gold," cotton is grown in 91 of Georgia's 159 counties. It is the most widespread of any row crop grown in Georgia.

SNICKERDOODLES

1	cup butter or shortening
1½	cups sugar
2	eggs
2 ⅔	cups flour
2	teaspoons cream of tartar
1	teaspoon baking soda
¼	teaspoon salt
2	tablespoons sugar
2	teaspoons cinnamon

Cream shortening, butter, sugar and egg thoroughly. Sift together flour, cream of tartar, soda, and salt. Add to the creamed mixture. Roll into balls the size of a small walnut. Mix sugar and cinnamon together and roll balls in mixture. Place 2 inches apart on ungreased cooking sheet. Bake at 400 degrees for 8 to 10 minutes until light brown but soft. Cookies will be crisp when cool. Cool on wire racks. Yield: 4 dozen

Nancy Coleman
Hartsfield, Georgia

In 2006, Georgia ranked second in the nation in cotton acreage; it had about 1.4 million acres with an estimated value of $745 million.

PECAN KISSES

1	egg white
½	teaspoon vanilla extract
¾	cup light brown sugar
2	cups chopped pecans

Beat egg white until stiff. Add all ingredients. Drop on well greased cookie sheet. Bake at 250 degrees for 30 minutes. Turn oven off and let kisses remain in over 30 minutes longer. Remove from oven and let cool. Store in tightly covered container. Pecan Kisses will keep in a cool place for a week.

Patsy Wester
Meigs, Georgia

CHRISTMAS COOKIES

½	cup margarine
½	cup sugar
1	egg
3	cups all-purpose flour
¼	teaspoon salt
3	teaspoons baking powder
½	cup milk
½	teaspoon vanilla extract
¼	teaspoon nutmeg

In a large mixing bowl, cream margarine until fluffy. Add sugar and egg until well blended. Add dry ingredients, milk and flavorings. Cover and chill for several hours, overnight is best. Using a rolling pin, roll cookie dough out on floured surface. Cut into desired shapes. Bake 350 degrees for 8 to 10 minutes. Cool on racks.

Tracey Abrams
Jackson, Mississippi

BUTTER COOKIES

1	cup butter
1	cup sugar
1	egg
1	teaspoon vanilla extract
2	teaspoons baking powder
3	cups all-purpose flour

Colored sugar, optional

Preheat oven to 400 degrees. Cream butter and sugar together. Beat in egg and vanilla. Mix baking powder and flour; add one cup at a time to creamed mixture until stiff. Roll out dough onto floured/sugar surface. Cut into desired shapes. Place on cookie sheet lined with parchment paper. Add sugar crystals and press down into dough, if desired. Bake 7-10 minutes until golden brown.

Jane Gibbs
Moultrie, Georgia

TEA CAKES

3	cups self-rising flour
1 ¼	cups sugar
2	eggs
½	cup butter
1	teaspoon vanilla extract
1	tablespoon milk

Cream sugar and butter. Add eggs, vanilla, milk. Add sifted flour and mix well. Chill in refrigerator for several hours. Roll into balls and flatten with sugar dipped glass or roll out and use cookie cutter. Bake on ungreased cookie sheet at 375 degrees until light brown on bottom. Do not over bake.

Patsy Wester
Meigs, Georgia

SUGAR COOKIES

(A first edition favorite)

1	cup sugar
½	cup (1 stick) butter
1	egg
1	teaspoon vanilla
2	cups all-purpose flour
½	teaspoon salt
1	teaspoon baking powder

Cream sugar and butter; add egg and vanilla. Sift flour, salt and baking powder. Add to creamed mixture. Chill 1 hour. (Hint: Leave dough not being used in refrigerator. It is easier to cut when cold.) Roll out on a floured board. (I add ¼ cup granulated sugar with the flour.) Cut and bake on ungreased cookie sheet in a preheated 375 degrees oven for 8 minutes. Yield: 2 dozen.

Perfect for cutting and decorating. Randolph makes these a lot.

Jane Gibbs
Moultrie, Georgia

MAMA WOLF'S TEA CAKES

(A first edition favorite)

2	eggs
1	cup sugar
½	cup shortening
1	teaspoon vanilla
	Self-rising flour

Beat eggs and sugar; add shortening and mix well. Add vanilla and as much flour as needed to make a soft dough. Roll out and cut with a cookie or biscuit cutter. Cook at 350 degrees until brown.

Linda West
Byromville, Georgia

Cookies

LEMON MUFFINS

1   yellow cake mix and ingredients listed on box
1   (3 ounce) package lemon gelatin
1   cup hot water
1   (12 ounce) can lemonade concentrate, thawed
2   cups confectioner's sugar, sifted

Dissolve gelatin in hot water. Mix cake according to package directions substituting gelatin dissolved in hot water for water on package directions. Spray mini-muffin pans with non-stick spray and fill about half full with batter. Bake at 350 degrees until just done, about 10 minutes (don't allow to brown). To speed up the baking process, bake four muffin pans at once. While baking, dissolve sugar in lemonade concentrate (do not add water). When muffins are done, remove from pan and dip in lemonade mixture. Place on cake rack with wax paper underneath to catch drips. Allow to set for a few minutes to absorb mixture. Store in airtight container. Place wax paper between layers. Can be frozen. Yield: about 100

A little time-consuming but worth it. A gentleman once commented that they had enough pucker power to make you want to kiss your sister.

Nancy Coleman
Hartsfield, Georgia

Many recipes call for a 1-pound box of powdered sugar. However, some stores only carry 2-pound bags. A 1-pound box of powdered sugar contains about 4 ½ cups, sifted.

Cookies

PECAN TASSIES

1	cup butter, softened
1	(8-ounce) package cream cheese, softened
2 ½	cups all-purpose flour
1 ½	cups brown sugar, packed
1 ½	cups chopped pecans
2	large eggs
2	tablespoons butter, melted
2	teaspoons vanilla extract
⅛	teaspoon salt

Beat 1 cup butter and cream cheese at medium speed with electric mixer until creamy. Gradually add flour to butter mixture, beating at low speed. Shape mixture into 48 balls and place on baking sheet; cover and chill 1 hour. Place 1 dough ball into each lightly greased cup of mini muffin pans, pressing in bottom and up sides of cup. Whisk together brown sugar, pecans, eggs, water, vanilla and salt. Spoon into pastry shells. Bake 350 degrees for 20 minutes or until filling is set. Cool in pans on wire racks 10 minutes. Remove from pans; cool on wire rack 20 minutes or until completely cool.

Vickie Abrams
Berlin, Georgia

The extensive cotton industry in Georgia includes farming, ginning, cottonseed oil mills, textile mill processing, warehousing, and selling cotton. It contributes an estimated $1.4 billion annually to Georgia's economy and provides employment for over 11,700 Georgians.

THUMBPRINT COOKIES

2 cups all-purpose flour
¾ cup powdered sugar
1 cup margarine
1 teaspoon vanilla
1 cup chopped nuts
Jelly, your favorite flavor

Mix first 5 ingredients, shape into small balls, and stick your little finger in the center to make a hole for the jelly. Drop just enough jelly in to fill the hole and bake at 350 degrees for 10 minutes.

Always a favorite!

Cathy Thompson
Vienna, Georgia

Desserts and Pies

THE BOLL WEEVIL

Of all the dreaded, destructive insects in North America, none was more feared in the cotton belt than the boll weevil. It first entered the U.S. from Mexico around 1900 and made its way across the South to Georgia. The little gray beetle with a long snout feeds on the newly-developed cotton boll, destroying its growth.

By 1921 it had swept the entire state. The average yield dropped from 252 pounds per acre in 1914 to 106 pounds per acre in 1923. Weevil damage reached a peak in 1925. In Georgia, the boll weevil was responsible for millions of dollars worth of damage. It is estimated that a single boll weevil can destroy enough cotton in one day to make a man's shirt.

The Boll Weevil Eradication Program was implemented in Georgia in 1987. It has lowered production costs, provided conditions for an increased yield of cotton per acre and reduced the use of pesticides by 90 percent. The program was so successful that in 1995, the boll weevil was officially declared "dead" in Georgia.

As a result, cotton production grew from an all-time low of 115,000 acres in 1978 to1.4 million acres in 2006. Once again, cotton was king in Georgia.

INDEX

Desserts and Pies

BLUEBERRY CRUNCH

(A first edition favorite)

1	(20-ounce) can crushed pineapple, with juice
1	pint blueberries, washed
2	tablespoons lemon juice
½	cup sugar
1	box yellow cake mix
1	cup chopped nuts
¼	cup sugar
½	cup (1 stick) melted margarine

Preheat oven to 350 degrees. Lightly grease 13x9-inch baking dish. Pour crushed pineapple with juice into dish. Lightly crush blueberries and mix with ½ cup sugar and lemon juice. Place blueberries over pineapple. Sprinkle dry cake mix over berries. Mix ¼ cup sugar and nuts. Sprinkle over cake mix. Pour melted margarine over nuts and cake mix. Bake 20 minutes then cut with knife to allow juice to rise to the top. Bake 30 minutes longer. May take a little longer in your oven. If nuts appear to be browning too much cover lightly with foil until cooking time is complete. Serve warm with whipped topping or ice cream.

This is my mother's favorite blueberry dessert and we even love it right out of the refrigerator—if there was any left the first time. Great for cover dish dinners.

Nancy Coleman
Hartsfield, Georgia

CRUNCHY APPLE CAKE

1	(21-ounce) can apple pie filling
1	box white or yellow cake mix
1	stick butter, melted
1	cup chopped pecans

Spread pie filing in bottom of 8-inch square baking pan. Sprinkle dry cake mix over filling. Pour melted butter over cake mix; sprinkle with pecans. Bake at 375 degrees for 45 minutes or until top is brown.

Quick, easy and good. Serve warm topped with vanilla ice cream.

Vivian Morrison
Cusseta, Georgia

DUMP CAKE

1   yellow cake mix
1   can (20-ounce) crushed pineapple in syrup
1   can (21-ounce) cherry pie filling
1   cup chopped pecans
½   cup butter, cut in thin slices

Preheat oven to 350 degrees. Grease 13x9-inch pan. Dump undrained pineapple into pan; spread evenly. Dump in pie filling and spread into even layer. Dump dry cake mix onto cherry layer; spread evenly. Sprinkle pecans over cake mix. Put butter on top. Bake for 45-50 minutes. Serve warm or cooled.

Mary Barber
Tifton, Georgia

CHERRY CINNAMON COBBLER

1   (21-ounce) can cherry pie filling
1   (12.4-ounce) package refrigerated cinnamon rolls

Spread pie filling into a greased 8-inch square baking dish. Set icing aside. Arrange rolls in baking dish. Bake at 400 degrees for 15 minutes. Cover and bake 10 minutes longer or until golden brown. Remove from oven. Spread icing over rolls. Serve warm. Ready in 30 minutes or less. Yield: 8 servings

Cary Hart Deas
Berlin, Georgia

EASY FRUIT COBBLER

½ cup flour
1   teaspoon baking powder
½ cup milk
½ cup sugar
2   cups peaches, blueberries or blackberries, sweetened to taste
¼ cup butter, melted

Mix flour, baking powder, sugar and milk. Place fruit in a 2-quart baking dish. Pour mixture over fruit; top with melted butter and bake 30-45 minutes at 400 degrees. It makes its own crust. Yield: 4-6 servings.

Tonya Loraine Bustle
Coolidge, Georgia

EASY FRUIT PIE

(A first edition favorite)

1   cup self-rising flour, sifted
1   cup milk
⅔ cup sugar
1   stick margarine
2   cups fresh peaches, pears, apples, etc.

Put flour, milk, sugar and ½ stick melted margarine in bowl, mix well by hand. Place in casserole dish; add fruit on top. Add rest of melted margarine on top. Bake at 375 degrees until crust browns. It makes its own crust. Yield: 6 to 8 servings. To make larger pie/cobbler, double pastry and fruit amounts.

Louise Milliron
Shellman, Georgia

FRESH BERRY PIE

(A first edition favorite)

1	package refrigerated pie crusts (2 crusts)
4	cups fresh blueberries or blackberries, washed and picked for stems
4	teaspoons lemon juice
¾	cup sugar
¼	cup all-purpose flour
½	teaspoon ground cinnamon
¼	teaspoon nutmeg
⅛	teaspoon salt
2	tablespoons margarine

Fit one pie crust into a 9-inch pie plate, according to package directions. Fold edges under and crimp. Set aside remaining crust. Gently mix berries in bowl with lemon juice. Mix dry ingredients and add to berries. Toss gently. Turn into the unbaked pie shell, heaping slightly at center. Dot with margarine. Complete as for two crust pie, following package directions. Cover edges with narrow strip of foil to prevent over browning. Bake at 450 degrees for 10 minutes. Reduce heat to 350 degrees and bake for 30 to 35 minutes or until crust is lightly browned. Set on wire rack to cool. Serve with whipped topping or ice cream.

A long-time family favorite from my mother, Lois Clark.

Nancy Coleman
Hartsfield, Georgia

To prevent over browning the edge of a pie crust, cut a shield make of heavy duty foil. Before filling the pie pan with dough, turn the pie pan upside on foil and trace around the edge. Cut about ¾ inch inside and outside the mark creating a circle about 1½ -inch wide. Once the pie is ready to place in the oven, lightly cover the edge with the foil circle.

Desserts and Pies

PEAR PIE

(A first edition favorite)

1¼   cups sugar
¼   teaspoon salt
½   teaspoon cinnamon
4   tablespoons flour
6-8   pears, peeled, cored and sliced thin
1   teaspoon vanilla extract
¼   cup butter
Pastry for 2 crust pie

Fit one pie crust into a 9-inch pie plate, according to package directions. Fold edges under and crimp. Set aside remaining crust. Combine sugar, salt, cinnamon, and flour in a small mixing bowl; mix well. Pour half of sugar mixture evenly over pastry. Add pears; sprinkle vanilla on top of pears. Sprinkle remaining sugar over pears. Dot with butter. Cover with top crust; fold edge of top crust under edge of bottom crusts. Seal and flute edges. Make slits in several places to allow steam to escape. Bake at 350 degrees for 15 minutes. Reduce heat to 300 degrees and continue baking for 40 minutes or until light brown. If pears are hard, precook for a little while in a very small amount of water.

I thought pear pie was as common as apple pie until I was teaching in Albany and friends said they had never eaten pear pie. I prepared this recipe on "Town and County" on WALB-TV and had more comments on it than any other recipe I have prepared on the show.

Nancy Coleman
Hartsfield, Georgia

FRIED APPLE TARTS

1   (6-ounce) bag dried apples
2   cups sugar
3   cups water
2   (10 each) cans large biscuits

Cook apples in water until tender. Add sugar and cook until juice thickens. Drain juice from apples. Refrigerate apples overnight to make them firm and easier to work with. Roll biscuits flat. Put 1 tablespoon of apples in center of each biscuit. Fold one side of biscuit over apples and crimp edges of biscuit with fork to seal. Have all tarts made before you start frying. Fry in hot grease over low heat. Use enough grease so tarts will float and not burn. Turn tarts over once in grease and brown on both sides. Drain on paper towels. Dust with powdered sugar, if desired.

My husband's uncle was famous for his Apple Tarts. I make them in Uncle T's memory for the family fish fry on Labor Day weekend. They are gone as soon as they hit the table. They may as well be an appetizer as they are the first thing eaten.

Nancy Coleman,
Hartsfield, Georgia

COCONUT PIE
(A first edition favorite)

½   cup (1 stick) margarine, melted
1   cup sugar
1   tablespoon white vinegar
3   eggs
1   teaspoon vanilla extract
1   heaping cup coconut
1   9-inch refrigerated pie crust, uncooked

Combine all ingredients and mix well. Fit pie crust into a 9-inch pie plate, according to package directions. Fold edges under and crimp. Pour filling into crust. Bake at 350 degrees for 45 to 50 minutes or until done. Yield: 8 servings

It is simple to make two pies at once with this recipe. I used the refrigerated pie crust. Very good and easy. It gets raves every time I make it.

Nancy Coleman
Hartsfield, Georgia

Desserts and Pies

CHOCOLATE PECAN PIE

1	cup evaporated milk
3	tablespoons margarine
6	ounces chocolate chips
3	ounces butterscotch chips
3	eggs, beaten
1 ½	cups sugar
3	tablespoons flour
2	teaspoons vanilla extract
2	cups chopped pecans
2	unbaked pie crusts

Heat milk and margarine. Add chips and stir until melted. Mix eggs, sugar, flour, vanilla and pecans together. Add to chocolate mixture. Pour into pie crusts. Bake at 350 degrees for 35 minutes. Yield: 2 pies, 8 servings each

Given to me by my close friend, Janet Whittle. This has become a favorite of ours.

Jane Gibbs
Moultrie, Georgia

Linters – the short fuzz on the seed – provide cellulose for making plastics, rocket propellants, rayon, pharmaceutical emulsions, cosmetics, photography and x-ray film, and upholstery.

WALNUT FUDGE PIE

3   large eggs, slightly beaten
½   cup firmly packed brown sugar
¼   cup all-purpose flour
¼   cup butter or margarine, melted
1   teaspoon vanilla extract
1   (12-ounce) package semisweet chocolate chips, melted
1 ½   cups walnut or pecan pieces
½   (15-ounce) package refrigerated pie crusts
Coffee ice cream
Java Chocolate Sauce

Stir together eggs, brown sugar, flour, butter and vanilla until blended; stir in melted chocolate chips and nuts. Fit pie crusts into a 9-inch pie plate, according to package directions. Fold edges under and crimp. Spoon chocolate filling into crust. Bake at 375 degrees for 30 minutes. Cool completely on a wire rack. Serve with coffee ice cream and, if desired, Java Chocolate Sauce. Yield: 8 servings.

Java Chocolate Sauce
1   (12-ounce) package semisweet chocolate chips
½   cup whipping cream
1   tablespoon butter or margarine
¼   cup strong brewed coffee

Heat chocolate chips, cream and butter in a heavy saucepan over low heat until chocolate and butter melt, stirring often. Cook, stirring constantly, 2 to 3 minutes or until smooth. Remove form heat; stir in coffee. Serve warm. Yield: 1 ¼ cups

This pie with the sauce is almost chocolate overload, but so good with ice cream. The sauce is good on ice cream with the pie is all gone. Try stirring the sauce into milk, hot or cold.

Nancy Coleman
Hartsfield, Georgia

Desserts and Pies

MARY'S GRAHAM CRACKER PECAN PIE

3	egg whites
1	cup sugar
1 ½	cup crushed graham crackers
1 ½	cup chopped pecans
½	teaspoon baking powder
½	teaspoon vanilla flavoring

Beat egg whites and baking powder together until still peaks form; add sugar slowly; add vanilla. Fold in crumbs slowly; add pecans. Pour in greased 9-inch pie dish. Bake for 30 minutes at 350 degrees. For a moist pie, cover and store in the refrigerator.

You can serve pie with whipped cream or Cool Whip.

Mary Walker
Tifton, Georgia

GRANDMOTHER NETTIE'S PECAN PIE

1	(1-pound) box light brown sugar
1	stick margarine, melted
3	eggs
3	tablespoons milk
3	tablespoons self-rising flour
1	teaspoon vanilla extract
1	cup chopped pecans
2	9-inch pie crusts, unbaked

Mix all ingredients and pour into two pie crusts. Bake at 350° for 45-55 minutes.

Patsy Wester
Meigs, Georgia

PECAN PIE

(A first edition favorite)

3 eggs, beaten slightly
1 cup dark corn syrup
½ cup granulated sugar
1 teaspoon vanilla
Dash of salt
1 cup nuts, chopped
1 (8 or 9-inch) pie crust

Combine first five ingredients and mix thoroughly; add nuts. Pour into an unbaked pie shell. Bake in a preheated oven at 325 degrees for about 50 minutes, or until set in middle.

This is my mother's recipe. I've never tasted one better.

Virginia Hart
Moultrie, Georgia

CHRISTMAS PECAN PIE

½ cup (1 stick) butter
1 cup sugar
2 eggs, beaten
1 tablespoon white vinegar
½ cup coconut
½ cup golden raisins
1 cup pecans
Pinch of salt
1 unbaked pie crust

Melt butter. Mix sugar, salt, eggs, vinegar, coconut, raisins, pecans, and butter until well blended. Pour into the unbaked pie crust. Bake at 350 degrees 40-50 minutes until golden brown.

Mary Walker
Tifton, Georgia

Desserts and Pies

CHESS PIE

(A first edition favorite)

1	cup sugar	2	tablespoons corn meal
3	egg yolks	½	teaspoon lemon flavoring
½	cup cream	1	pie crust, baked
¼	cup butter		

Mix sugar, beaten egg yolks, cream, melted butter, corn meal and lemon flavoring; pour in baked pie crust.

Meringue: Add ¼ teaspoon cream of tartar to the 3 egg whites, beat until almost stiff enough to hold a peak. Add sugar gradually, beating until stiff but not dry. Pile lightly on pie filling and bake at 325 degrees for 40 to 45 minutes.

Sharon G. Turner
Pavo, Georgia

SWEET POTATO PIE

(A first edition favorite)

2	cups cooked, mashed sweet potatoes
½	cup softened margarine
2	eggs, separated
1	cup firmly packed brown sugar
¼	teaspoon salt
½	teaspoon ground ginger
½	teaspoon ground nutmeg
½	teaspoon ground cinnamon
½	cup milk
¼	cup sugar
1	9-inch unbaked deep-dish pan shell

Combine sweet potatoes, margarine, egg yolks, brown sugar, salt and spices; mix well. Add milk, blending until smooth. Beat egg whites until foamy, gradually add sugar, beating until stiff. Fold into sweet potato mixture. Pour into pie shell. Sprinkle with additional spices, if desired. Bake at 400 degrees for 10 minutes. Reduce heat to 350 degrees and bake 30 additional minutes. When cool, garnish with whipped cream and orange rind if desired. Yield: 6 to 8 servings.

Vickie Abrams
Berlin, Georgia

CREAMY CHEESECAKE

Vanilla Wafer crust:
- 30   vanilla wafers (may use graham crackers or ginger snaps)
- 1 to 2 hands-full of toasted, coarsely chopped, almonds,
      or any preferred nut (optional)
- 1   tablespoon melted butter
- Ground cinnamon
- Whole nutmeg, grated (optional)

Crumble the wafers in a processor or use a hand-crank cheese grater (this is really fast and easy). Chop or process the (optional) nuts to desired coarseness. Press the crumb-nut mixture firmly into the bottom of a 9-inch spring-form pan. Lightly drizzle melted butter, here-and-there, over the crumbs so they stay put when filling. Lightly sprinkle cinnamon and a VERY light (optional) grating of nutmeg. Distribute the desired amount of nuts on top. Place on a shallow baking pan and set aside. Preheat oven to 375 degrees.

Filling:
- 3   eggs
- 1 ½   cups sugar
- 1 ½   teaspoons vanilla extract
- 3   (8-ounce) packages cream cheese (**NOT SPREADABLE!**)

Have filling ingredients at room temperature. Beat eggs at high speed, adding sugar, vanilla and cream cheese. Mix thoroughly at medium speed until creamy. Gently pour onto the prepared crust. Sprinkle very lightly with cinnamon. Bake for 25 minutes. Allow to cool completely before applying the optional topping. Cover and refrigerate for at least 8 hours before serving

Optional Creamy Topping:
- 1 ½   cups sour cream
- 2   tablespoons sugar
- ½   teaspoon pure vanilla extract

Preheat oven to 400 degrees. Mix ingredients at medium speed. Spread onto the top of a completely cooled cake. Bake for 5 minutes. Cool for 1 hour before refrigerating as described above.

Karen Nikitopoulos
Georgia Cotton Commission
Perry, Georgia

Desserts and Pies

KEY LIME CHEESECAKE WITH STRAWBERRY BUTTER SAUCE

2	cups graham cracker crumbs
¼	cup sugar
½	cup butter, melted
3	(8 ounce) packages cream cheese
1¼	cups sugar
6	eggs, separated
1	(8-ounce) carton sour cream
1 ½	teaspoons grated lime rind
½	cup Key lime juice

Combine cracker crumbs, sugar and melted butter; firmly press on bottom and 1 inch up sides of buttered 9-inch spring form pan. Bake 350 degrees for 8 minutes. Cool. Beat cream cheese at medium speed until fluffy. Gradually add 1 ¼ cups sugar. Beat well. Add egg yolks one at a time beating after each. Stir in sour cream, lime rind and juice. Beat egg whites until stiff peaks form. Fold into cream cheese mixture. Pour over crust. Bake 350 degrees for 1 hour and turn off oven. Partially open door and leave in oven 15 minutes. Run knife around sides. Cool completely in pan on wire rack. Cover and chill 8 hours.

Strawberry Butter Sauce

1 ¼	cups fresh strawberries, hulled
¼	cup melted butter
½	cup sifted powdered sugar
1 ½	teaspoon grated lime rind

Process berries in food processor using knife blade until smooth. Stir in butter, powdered sugar and lime rind. Slice cheesecake and pour on sauce.

Brenda Morris
Ocilla, Georgia

TURTLE CHEESECAKE

Crust:

10	graham crackers, crushed (I use half low-fat, half regular)
¾	cup English toffee bits (such as Skor or Heath)
2 ½	tablespoons packed dark brown sugar
½	cup unsalted butter, melted

Preheat over to 350 degrees. Mix crushed graham crackers, toffee bits and dark brown sugar in a medium bowl. Add melted butter; stir until clumps form. Pour into a 10-inch spring form pan and press mixture up sides and then bottom. Bake until crust is set, about 10 minutes. Set aside. Turn oven off and leave open half way for 10 minutes to allow cool down. Turn oven back on at 325 degrees.

Filling:

3	(8-ounce) packages cream cheese, softened
1 ¼	cups granulated sugar
4	large eggs
1	(8-ounce) carton sour cream
1	tablespoon vanilla extract

Beat cream cheese at medium speed with an electric mixer until creamy; gradually add sugar, beating well. Stop mixer and scrape down sides with rubber scraper. Add eggs, one at a time, beating well after each addition and scraping sides and bottom as needed. Stop mixer and scrap down sides again. Stir in sour cream and vanilla. Pour batter into prepared crust. Bake at 325 degrees for 65 minutes. Center will not be completely set. Turn over off; open oven door half way. Leave cheesecake in oven for 1 hour. Remove to wire rack to completely cool. Cover and chill at least 8 hours before removing from pan. If you plan on freezing it, cover and put in freezer in spring form pan. Let freeze 24 hours. Take out and remove pan. Run a spatula under crust to loosen. Place on a cardboard round and wrap securely in plastic wrap and place back in freezer. Take out of freezer 12 hours before serving.

Mandy Wingate Kinsey
Moultrie, Georgia

CANDIED APPLE CHEESECAKE

1	cup crushed ginger snaps
3	tablespoons butter, melted
½	cup plus 2 tablespoons sugar, divided
2	(8-ounce) packages cream cheese, softened
2	teaspoons vanilla extract
½	cup sour cream
2	eggs
1	cup apple pie filling, divided
½	cup pecan pieces, divided
½	cup toffee bits, divided

Heat oven to 325 degrees. Mix ginger snaps crumbs, butter and 2 tablespoons sugar; press onto bottom and up side of 9- inch pie plate. Beat cream cheese, ½ cup sugar and vanilla with mixer until blended. Add sour cream; mix well. Add eggs, one at a time, beating after each just until blended. Stir in half of pie filling, half of nuts and half of toffee bits pour into crust. Bake 35 minutes or until center is almost set. Cool. Refrigerate 4 hours. Top with remaining pie filling, nuts and toffee bits right before serving.

Linda Stripling
Moultrie, Georgia

The first cotton mill in Georgia to convert cotton into fabric was the Bolton Factory, built in 1811, near Washington, Georgia.

JACQUELINE KENNEDY'S CRÈME BRULEE

6	egg yolks
6	teaspoons granulated sugar
3	cups heavy cream
¼	teaspoon vanilla extract
½	cup light brown sugar

Heat the heavy cream in a double boiler. In a large bowl, beat the egg yolks and granulated sugar until the mixture is light and creamy. Stir the warm cream into the egg yolk mixture very slowly. Return the mixture to double boiler and cook until the custard coats the spoon, stirring constantly. Add vanilla extract. Pour into a 2-quart heatproof casserole. Put in refrigerator and chill for several hours, or overnight. When ready to serve, sprinkle the brown sugar evenly over the top. Have your broiler preheated. Place the casserole in a pan of crushed ice, and place under the broiler until the sugar melts and caramelizes. Watch very carefully so that the sugar will not burn. Serve immediately. Yield: 6 servings

I got this recipe on a family vacation trip to Jacqueline Kennedy's childhood home, Hammersmith Farms in Newport, Rhode Island. It is delicious!

Charlotte Mathis
Moultrie, Georgia

Desserts and Pies

PUMPKIN PIE DESSERT SQUARES

Crust:
1	package yellow cake mix
½	cup margarine, melted
1	egg

Spray the bottom of a 13x9-inch pan. Reserve 1 cup cake mix for topping. Combine remaining cake mix, margarine, and egg. Press into pan.

Filling:
1	(1 pound, 14-ounce can) can pumpkin pie mix
2	eggs
⅔	cup milk

Mix all ingredients until smooth. Pour over cake mix crust.

Topping:
1	cup reserved cake mix
¼	cup brown sugar
1	teaspoon cinnamon
¼	cup margarine
½	cup chopped pecans

Combine all ingredients. Sprinkle over filling. Bake at 350 degrees for 45 minutes. Cool completely. Cut into squares and serve with whipped cream

Gail Thompson
Moultrie, Georgia

PECAN PIE BARS

Crust:

3	cups all-purpose flour
½	teaspoon salt
¾	cup sugar
1	cup cold butter

In a large bowl, combine flour, sugar and salt. Cut in butter until crumbly. Press into bottom and up the sides of a greased 15x10x1-inch baking pan. Bake at 350 degrees for 18-22 minutes or until crust edges are beginning to brown and bottom is set.

Filling:

4	eggs
1 ½	cups corn syrup
1 ½	teaspoons vanilla extract
1 ½	cups sugar
¼	cup butter, melted
2 ½	cups chopped pecans

Combine the eggs, sugar, corn syrup, butter and vanilla in a large bowl; mix well. Stir in pecans. Pour over crust. Bake 25-30 minutes or until edges are firm and center is almost set. Cool on wire racks. Cut into bars. Refrigerate until serving.

These bars taste just like an old fashioned pecan pie, just easier to eat. The Colquitt County Farm Bureau served these bars when Georgia Farm Bureau emphasized pecans as their chief commodity one year.

Charlotte Wingate
Doerun, Georgia

CARAMEL GLAZED APPLE SQUARES

1	cup vegetable oil
2	cups sugar
2	large eggs
2	teaspoons vanilla extract
3	cups all-purpose flour
½	teaspoon salt
1	teaspoon baking soda
1	teaspoon ground cinnamon
1	cup milk
3	cups peeled and diced apples
1	cup chopped pecans or walnuts

Combine oil and sugar and beat well. Beat in eggs and vanilla extract. Sift together flour, salt, soda and cinnamon. Add this alternately with the milk to the oil mixture. Fold in apples and nuts. Pour into a greased 9x13-inch baking dish. Bake at 325 degrees for 40-45 minutes until it tests done.

Caramel Glaze:

1	cup light brown sugar
½	cup butter or margarine
¼	cup evaporated milk
1	teaspoon vanilla extract

Heat sugar and butter or margarine until melted. Add milk and bring to a full boil. Cook one minute and add vanilla extract. Spread evenly over warm cake. Let cool and cut into 15-18 squares.

Jane Gibbs
Moultrie, Georgia

CHOCOLATE – PEANUT BUTTER MALLOW BARS

1   box devil's food cake mix
1   stick butter, melted
⅔   cup cold milk, divided in half
¾   cup creamy peanut butter
1   (7-ounce) jar marshmallow crème
½   cup salted peanuts
6   squares semisweet chocolate, coarsely chopped

Heat oven to 350 degrees. Mix dry cake mix, butter and 1/3 cup milk until blended; press two-thirds onto bottom of 13x9-inch pan. Bake 12-14 minutes or until center is almost set; cool for 3 minutes. Mix peanut butter and remaining milk; spread onto crust. Top with spoonfuls of marshmallow crème and remaining cake mixture. Sprinkle with nuts and chocolate; press gently into cake mixture. Bake 18 minutes or until center is set. Cool before cutting into bars.

Linda Stripling
Moultrie, Georgia

BUCKEYE BARS DESSERT

½   cup (1 stick) butter, softened
¾   cup crunchy peanut butter
22   vanilla wafers, crushed (¾ cup)
2   cups powdered sugar
½   (8-ounce) carton frozen whipped topping, do not thaw
3   (1 ounce) squares semisweet chocolate

Line 8-inch square pan with foil, with ends of foil extended over sides. Beat butter and peanut butter with mixer until blended. Add wafer crumbs; mix well. Gradually add sugar, mixing well after each addition. Press onto bottom of foil-lined pan. Microwave frozen whipped topping and chocolate in bowl on high 1 minute; stir. Microwave 15-30 seconds more to melt chocolate. Stir to blend. Spread over peanut butter layer. Refrigerate 2 hours. Use foil sides to lift from pan before cutting.

Linda Stripling
Moultrie, Georgia

Desserts and Pies

BLUE WILLOW SQUARES

1   (18.25 ounce) package yellow cake mix
½   cup (1 stick) butter or margarine, softened
1   cup chopped pecans
3   eggs, divided
1   (8-ounce) package cream cheese, softened
1   (1 pound) box powdered sugar

Preheat oven to 350 degrees. In a large mixing bowl, combine cake mix, butter, pecans and 1 egg by hand with spoon. Mix well. Press dough by hand into ungreased 8x11-inch baking pan. (Use ice water to chill your hands for easier handling.) In mixing bowl, lightly beat 2 remaining eggs. Add softened cream cheese and beat well. Add confectioners' sugar and blend. Mixture should be slightly lumpy. Spoon this over cake mixture and spread evenly. Bake for 35-40 minutes or until golden brown. Remove from oven and set aside to cool for 1 hour. Cut into squares for serving. Yield: about 20 servings.

This recipe is from "The Blue Willow Inn Bible of Southern Cooking".

Myra Kirksey
Byromville, Georgia

The American farmer produces the safest, most economical, most reliable and most abundant supply of food, fiber and fuel in the world.

GEORGIA PEACHES AND CREAM

(A first edition favorite)

2	cups all-purpose flour
¾	cup margarine, melted
1	cup chopped pecans
3	cups powdered sugar
1	(8-ounce) package cream cheese, softened
1	(9-ounce) container whipped topping
1	cup sugar
3	tablespoons cornstarch
1	cup water
1	(3-ounce) package peach gelatin
4	cups fresh peaches, peeled and sliced

Combine flour and margarine. Stir in chopped pecans. Press into a 9x13-inch baking dish. Bake at 350 degrees for about 10 minutes or until lightly browned. Cool, set aside. Mix powdered sugar with cream cheese until smooth; add whipped topping. Spoon on top of crust, pushing sides up to make a slight well for peaches. In a medium saucepan, mix sugar and cornstarch. Over medium heat slowly stir in water. Bring to boil, stirring constantly and cook one minute (scorches easily) until mixture is clear and slightly thickened. Remove from heat and add peach gelatin. Reserve ⅓ cup for peaches, spoon over cream mixture, leaving a one inch border of cream visible. Stir reserved glaze into peaches and spread on top. Refrigerate overnight or several hours. Variation: Strawberries and strawberry gelatin. Yields: 16 servings.

Wonderful and beautiful! This is my original recipe. It was featured in <u>Farm Journal</u> magazine.

Cathy Thompson
Pinehurst, GA

PEACH TRIFLE

(A first edition favorite)

1	(13½- inch) angel food cake
3	cups sliced peaches
1	(8-ounce) package low-fat cream cheese
1	can low-fat sweetened condensed milk
1	(12-ounce) carton reduced-calorie whipped topping

Break angel food cake into bite-size pieces. Peel and slice peaches; sprinkle with small amount of sugar. In mixing bowl, beat cream cheese, condensed milk and whipped topping. In a trifle dish or glass bowl, layer angel cake, peaches, then topping. Layer twice ending with topping. Prepare ahead and refrigerate.

The original recipe was a strawberry trifle, but we like peaches and they are available locally for a longer period of time. Of course, you can use products that are not low-fat or reduced-calorie, but we like it this way.

Virginia Hart
Moultrie, Georgia

STRAWBERRY CREAM PIE

(A first edition favorite)

1½	cup graham cracker crumbs
½	cup (1 stick) margarine, softened
1	(8-ounce) package cream cheese, softened to room temperature.
1	cup sugar
3	tablespoons milk
¾	cup chopped pecans
1	(12-ounce) container whipped topping
2	pints strawberries

Blend together graham cracker crumbs and margarine and pack firmly into 9x13-inch casserole dish. Blend cream cheese in blender. Then mix in sugar and milk. Spread over crust. Sprinkle chopped pecans over cheese mixture. Spread large whipped topping over nuts and top with strawberries cut in half with cut side down.

Julie Murphy*
Quitman, Georgia

Julie was one of the founders of Georgia Cotton Women and the first president.

STRAWBERRY DELIGHT

Crust:

1	cup all-purpose flour
½	cup margarine, softened
1	cup chopped pecans

Mix flour, margarine and pecans together. Press into a 9x13-inch baking dish. Bake at 350 degrees for 20-25 minutes. Cool.

Filling:

1	(12-ounce) carton whipped topping
1	cup powdered sugar
1	(8-ounce) package cream cheese

Mix all ingredients together and spread over cooled crust.

Topping:

1	pint fresh strawberries, washed, hulled and sliced
1	(3-ounce) box strawberry gelatin
1	cup hot water
¼	cup corn starch
1	cup sugar

Mix gelatin, water, corn starch and sugar together in saucepan. Cook over medium heat until mixture reaches full boil, stirring constantly. Reduce heat and cook about five minutes. Remove from heat. When cool, pour over strawberries and stir until well-coated. Pour strawberries over cream cheese filling. Refrigerate. When ready to serve, top with additional whipped topping and garnish with whole strawberries.

Nancy Coleman
Hartsfield, Georgia

Desserts and Pies

STRAWBERRY STUFF

2   (3-ounce) packages strawberry gelatin
2   cups boiling water
2   packages frozen sliced strawberries
1   (12-ounce) carton whipped topping
1   angel food cake

Mix gelatin in boiling water. Let it cool until it just begins to congeal. Add completely thawed strawberries and whipping topping to gelatin. Break angel food cake in small pieces. Using a 9x13-inch dish, layer of cake following with a layer of gelatin mixture. Repeat layers ending with gelatin mixture. Place in refrigerator to congeal. Serve in squares.

Cassandra Bullington
Cordele, Georgia

CHOCOLATE MOUSSE

1   (12-ounce) package semisweet chocolate chips
2   cups whipping cream
½   cup whipping cream
1   teaspoon vanilla extract
Whipped cream for garnish
Grated chocolate for garnish

In a medium-size glass bowl, microwave the chocolate chips and ½ cup whipping cream on high for 1½ minutes or until chocolate is melted, stirring every 30 seconds. Stir in the vanilla extract, blending well. Cool for 5 minutes. In a medium-size bowl with an electric mixer on medium speed, beat the remaining 2 cups of whipping cream until soft peaks form. Gently fold the whipped cream into the chocolate mixture. Spoon into a large serving bowl or individual dessert dishes. Garnish with additional whipped cream and grated chocolate, if desired. Chill two hours. Yield: 6-8 servings.

A light and luscious dessert. To make spooning mousse into parfait glasses easier, spoon mixture into gallon ziptop bag. Cut a small hole in one corner of the bag and squeeze the mousse into the glasses. For convenience, top with prepared whipped topping in a can with a nozzle, such as Redi-Whip.

Nancy Coleman
Hartsfield, Georgia

LAURA'S FROZEN CARAMEL PIES

(A first edition favorite)

1   (8-ounce) package cream cheese
1   can sweetened condensed milk
1   (16-ounce) carton whipped topping
⅔   cup pecans, toasted
⅔   cup coconut, toasted
3   graham cracker pie crusts
Caramel ice cream topping for drizzling

Beat cream cheese and condensed milk until smooth. Stir in whipped topping. Divide half the mixture between 3 pie shells. Sprinkle half of the nuts and half of the toasted coconut on cream cheese mixture. Drizzle caramel all around. Repeat with another layer ending with caramel. Keep frozen until just before using. Yield: 3 pies, 8 servings each

Judy Mobley
Moultrie, Georgia

LEMON PIE

1   (14-ounce) can sweetened condensed milk
1   (8-ounce) carton frozen whipped topping, thawed
½   cup lemon juice
2   drops yellow food coloring (optional)
1   9-inch graham cracker crust

In a medium bowl, combine condensed milk and juice. Let stand a few minutes. Stir in whipped topping. Add food coloring if desired. Spoon into crust. Chill until firm. Yield: 6 servings.

Vivian Morrison
Cusseta, Georgia

PEANUT BUTTER CREAM PIE

(A first edition favorite)

1	(8-ounce) package cream cheese, softened
¾	cup powdered sugar
½	cup creamy peanut butter
6	tablespoons milk
1	(8-ounce) carton whipped topping, thawed
1	9-inch graham cracker crust
¼	cup chopped peanuts

In a mixing bowl, beat cream cheese until fluffy. Add sugar and peanut butter. Mix well. Gradually add milk. Fold in whipped topping. Spoon into crust. Decorate with chopped peanuts. Chill for several hours or overnight. Yield: 6 servings

Easy to make. No baking required!

Lynn Tillman
Quitman, Georgia

YOGURT PIE

1	(12-ounce) carton whipped topping
2	(8-ounce) cartons peach yogurt (can substitute any flavor)
1	(15-ounce) can sliced peaches, drained
1	graham cracker crust

Mix together whipped topping, yogurt, and peaches. Pour into pie crust and freeze. Take out of freezer 20-30 minutes before serving and decorate the top with sliced peaches. Serve. Yield: 8 servings

Mary Walker
Tifton, Georgia

FIVE ALIVE PIE

1   can sweetened condensed milk
1   small can Five Alive frozen juice concentrate
1   large carton whipped topping
1   graham cracker crust

Mix together condensed milk, juice and whipped topping. Pour into graham cracker pie shell. Refrigerate 3 hours before serving.

Cassandra Bullington
Cordele, Georgia

RICH ICE CREAM
(A first edition favorite)

4   eggs
2   cups sugar
1   (12-ounce) can evaporated milk, chilled
1   (8-ounce) carton whipping cream
1   (14-ounce) can sweetened condensed milk
2   teaspoons vanilla extract
Homogenized milk

Beat eggs with electric mixer until very light and fluffy; gradually add sugar. Mix in evaporated milk, condensed milk, whipping cream, and vanilla; pour into freezer container and add enough milk to reach "fill" line on container. Stir with long-handled spoon. Freeze. Remove dasher and pack. Let ripen for at least 1 hour.

Note: For 6-quarts, use 6 eggs and 3 cups sugar.

Variation: Add 4 cups sweetened peaches or strawberries before pouring into freezer container.

When I was teaching foods, I used this recipe in my classes to demonstrate the various kinds of milk. The dairy unit was always a favorite with my students.

Nancy Coleman
Hartsfield, Georgia

Desserts and Pies

JIM'S CHOCOLATE HOMEMADE ICE CREAM

1   can evaporated milk
2   cups sugar
2   (3-ounce) boxes instant chocolate pudding mix
1   teaspoon vanilla flavoring
Milk - add as much as needed to fill the freezer

Mix all ingredients well, pour into freezer and freeze. Yield: 8 to 10 servings.

Louise Milliron
Shellman, Georgia

Cottonseed is crushed in order to separate its three products – oil, meal and hulls. Cottonseed oil is used primarily for shortening, cooking oil and salad dressing. It is used extensively in the snack food industry.

TAMMY'S KEY LIME PIE

1   (14-ounce) can fat-free sweetened condensed milk
¾   cup egg beaters
½   cup lime juice
    Graham cracker crust

Mix in blender. Pour in a low fat graham cracker crust. Bake at 350 degrees for 10 – 12 minutes. Refrigerate 2 hours.

Delicious and almost fat free!

Tammy Thompson Morgan
Charlotte, North Carolina

Entrees

THE MECHANIZATION OF COTTON

On a plantation near Savannah in the late 1700's, Eli Whitney, a Massachusetts teacher visiting the area, eliminated the tedious and costly task of separating cotton lint from the seed with his invention of the cotton gin (short for engine). This simple, hand-operated device patented in 1793, separated up to 50 pounds of lint from seed per day. This was a drastic improvement considering it previously required an individual an entire day to separate one pound. The gin replaced the work of 50 men. The invention was considered so significant to America's economy that the patent issued to Whitney was signed by the President of the United States, George Washington.

The next machine to revolutionize cotton was the mechanical cotton picker. A labor-intensive, back-breaking job, picking cotton had always been done by hand. Each fluffy white boll was pulled from its sharp burr. By the end of the day, hands were cut and bleeding. In the late 1940's, the sight of hunched-over bodies was replaced by machines stretching across the horizon. With the introduction of the mechanical cotton picker, growers could harvest their crops in a fraction of the time it took by hand.

Another invention that tremendously aids in harvesting cotton is the module builder. This machine packs cotton into large modules which look like loaves of bread. Each module holds 13 to 15 bales – each weighing about 500 pounds – or about 3.5 tons. Modules allow the cotton to be stored for a longer period of time before ginning without sacrificing yield or quality.

INDEX

JULIE'S ENGLISH MUFFIN PIZZAS

4   English muffins, split
1   cup pizza sauce
1   cup shredded Mozzarella cheese
½   cup shredded Parmesan cheese

Toast English muffin halves in a toaster. Top with pizza sauce, Mozzarella cheese, and Parmesan cheese. Place muffin halves in microwave and cook for 1 minute until cheese starts to melt.

Julie Anne Tyus
Moultrie, Georgia

CHEESY JOES

1   pound ground beef
1   onion, chopped
Salt, pepper and seasoned salt to taste
½   pound Velveeta
4   hamburger buns or other sandwich rolls

Brown ground beef and onion in skillet sprayed with cooking spray or a small amount of olive oil. Drain excess fat. Season to taste. Cut Velveeta into small cubes and add to ground beef, stirring constantly until melted. Spoon on to buns. Yield: 4 servings.

A cheesy version of sloppy joes.

Nancy Coleman
Hartsfield, Georgia

MEAT LOAF

½   cup catsup
2   tablespoons brown sugar
½   teaspoon dry mustard

Combine and mix together. Reserve four tablespoons for topping. Mix the remaining with:

4   teaspoons Worcestershire sauce
2   teaspoons season salt
1   onion, finely chopped
¼   teaspoon garlic powder
¼   teaspoon ground black pepper
1   egg
2   tablespoons chopped green pepper
1½   cups Wheat Chex or other bread or cracker crumbs
1½   pounds ground beef

Shape into loaf and place on sprayed baking pan. Bake at 350 degrees for 45 minutes. Spread remaining catsup mixture on top. Bake additional 15 minutes. Yield: 4-6 servings.

Brenda Chandler
Hull, Georgia

QUICK AND EASY MEATLOAF

1   (8-ounce) can cream of mushroom soup
2   pounds ground beef
1   envelope dry onion soup mix
½   cup dry bread crumbs
1   egg, beaten
¼   cup water

Mix thoroughly ½ cup of mushroom soup, beef, onion soup mix, bread crumbs, and egg. In 12x8-inch pan, firmly shape meat mixture into 8x4-inch loaf. Bake at 350 degrees for 1¼ hours. Spoon off 2 tablespoons drippings; reserve drippings. In saucepan over medium heat, heat remaining soup, water, and reserved drippings to boiling, stirring occasionally. Spoon over meatloaf. Yield: 8 servings.

Mary Walker
Tifton, Georgia

QUICK AND EASY SUPPER

1   pound ground beef
½   onion, chopped
1   stalk celery, chopped
1   (8-ounce) can peas and carrots
2-3 large potatoes, peeled and cubed
2   tablespoons flour
2   tablespoons oil
Salt and pepper to taste

Boil potatoes until almost done, drain (reserve liquid) and set aside. In a large skillet brown beef and drain. Add chopped onion and celery and cook until tender. At this point you make your own gravy using the oil and flour or use a package mix. Add browned beef mixture, peas and carrots and potatoes. Add liquid from potatoes as needed. Mix well adding salt and pepper to taste. Bring back to a slow simmer and simmer until potatoes are cooked completely.

Serve with hot biscuits or rolls. You can substitute vegetables that your family prefers.

Vickie Hart Abrams
Berlin, Georgia

HAMBURGER AND CABBAGE CASSEROLE

1   head cabbage, cut into quarters
4   cups water
1   pound ground beef
2   cups sour cream
1   (8-ounce) package Cheddar cheese, shredded

Preheat oven to 375 degrees. Spray a 9x13-inch baking dish or pan with cooking spray; set aside. Bring water to boil in a saucepan; add cabbage. Cook cabbage until tender; drain. In a skillet, brown the ground beef; drain. In a large mixing bowl, combine cabbage, ground beef, sour cream and cheese, reserving ¼ cup to sprinkle on top. Pour mixture into the baking dish and top with remaining cheese. Bake for 30-45 minutes, until bubbly. Remove from the oven and let stand about 10 minutes before serving.

Charlotte Wingate
Doerun, Georgia

SPAGHETTI SAUCE WITH BEEF

1	pound ground beef
1	tablespoon olive oil
1	onion, chopped
1	large clove garlic, minced (more is better)
1	bell pepper, chopped
1	jalapeño pepper, chopped (optional)
1	(28-ounce) can crushed tomatoes
1	(14-ounce) can diced tomatoes
¾	cup water
1	teaspoon sugar
1	teaspoon salt
1	teaspoon basil
1	teaspoon oregano
½	teaspoon pepper

In a large frying pan, heat oil over medium-high heat. Add onion, ground beef, bell pepper, jalapeño pepper and garlic. Cook until meat is brown; drain on paper towels to remove as much fat as possible. Return meat to frying pan and add remaining ingredients; bring to boil. Reduce heat. Cover and simmer, stirring occasionally, for 40 minutes as time allows. Serve over cooked spaghetti noodles. Yield: 6-8 servings

So much better than bottled sauces.

Nancy Coleman
Hartsfield, Georgia

Dried herbs are more potent than fresh — 3 teaspoons of fresh herbs equal 1 teaspoon dried herbs.

Entrees

TACO CASSEROLE

1	pound ground beef
1	cup salsa
½	package taco seasoning
½	cup milk
1	small onion, chopped
6	flour tortillas cut into 1-in pieces
1	green pepper, chopped
1	can condensed tomato soup
1 ½	cups grated cheese

Brown ground beef and add taco seasoning. Lightly sauté onion and green pepper with beef. Put mixture in mixing bowl. Add soup, salsa, milk, tortillas and 1 cup cheese. Bake in 9 x11-inch casserole dish at 400 degrees for 30 minutes. Sprinkle with ½ cup cheese.

Shredded cooked chicken breast is another excellent option!

Yvonne H. Crawford
Tifton, Georgia

HAMBURGER NOODLE SURPRISE CASSEROLE

1	large onion, chopped
1	large bell pepper, chopped
3	tablespoons bacon drippings
1	pound ground beef
1	can cream of mushroom soup
1	soup can of milk
1	can English peas
1	(15-ounce) package egg noodles, cooked and drained

Sauté onions and peppers in bacon drippings until tender, but not brown. Add ground meat and cook until mixture falls apart. Add remaining ingredients. Pour into a greased baking dish. Bake at 325 degrees for 1 hour. Yield: 8 servings.

Vivian Morrison
Cusseta, Georgia

SHEPHERD'S PIE

(A first edition favorite)

1 or 2 medium onions, chopped
1 green pepper, chopped (optional)
Cooking oil
1 to 1½ pounds lean ground beef
Salt and pepper
Garlic powder
6 to 8 potatoes, cooked and mashed
Butter and milk to taste
Grated cheese
Paprika

Sauté onions and green pepper in small amount of oil. Add ground beef and salt, pepper, garlic powder, and lemon pepper. Brown beef and drain. Mash potatoes and add butter, milk, and salt to taste. Potatoes should be a little stiff. Place meat in bottom of baking dish. Add potatoes to top. Sprinkle with grated cheese and paprika. Bake at 400 degrees about 30 minutes or until golden brown. Serve with green vegetables or salad. If you're in a hurry, use instant potatoes. Yield: 4-6 servings

My family loves this. When Clark was little, he loved it because it has two of his favorite foods—hamburger and "mashed tatas."

Nancy Coleman
Hartsfield, Georgia

154

CROCKPOT LASAGNA

1	pound ground beef
1	(4½-ounce) jar mushrooms
1	teaspoon dried Italian seasoning
1	(15-ounce) carton Ricotta or cottage cheese
1	(28-ounce) jar spaghetti sauce
2	cups shredded Mozzarella cheese, divided
⅓	cup water
8	lasagna noodles, uncooked

Cook beef and Italian seasoning in a large skillet over medium-high heat, stirring until beef crumbles, drain. Combine spaghetti sauce and water in a small bowl. Place 4 uncooked noodles in bottom of a lightly greased 5-quart electric slow cooker. Layer with half each of beef mixture, spaghetti sauce mixture and mushrooms. Spread ricotta or cottage cheese over mushrooms. Sprinkle with 1 cup mozzarella cheese. Repeat layer. Cover and cook on high setting 1 hour. Reduce heat to low until ready to serve.

Yvonne H. Crawford
Chula, Georgia

PRIME RIB

(A first edition favorite)

1	(8-pound) standing rib roast

Salt and pepper

Rub roast with salt and pepper. Place roast fat side up on a shallow roasting pan, uncovered. Place meat thermometer. Bake in a 325 degree oven for about 3¾ hours or 20 minutes per pound. Allow to stand for 20 minutes before carving.

Horseradish Sauce:

1	cup sour cream
⅓	cup prepared horseradish
1	teaspoon dill weed
1	teaspoon salt
¼	teaspoon pepper

Mix all ingredients. Chill for at least 3 hours. Serve with roast.

Thomas Coleman
Hartsfield, Georgia

SLOW-COOKED ROAST
(A first edition favorite)

1   (3 to 5 pound) beef roast
1   envelope onion soup mix
1 or 2 large onions, sliced
1   (10 ¾ ounce) can cream of mushroom soup

Coat crock pot with cooking spray. Mix cream of mushroom soup with onion soup mix. Place roast, which has been salted and peppered if desired, in crock pot. Pour soup mixture over roast. Top with sliced onions. Cook on low for 10 to 12 hours or on high for 5 to 6 hours. If you don't have a crock pot, place roast on large piece of heavy duty foil, pour soup mixture over roast and top with onions. Close foil tightly and place roast in large skillet. Cook at 250 degrees until done, about 5 to 6 hours. Yield: 6-8 servings.

This roast practically melts in your mouth. Even the not-so-tender cuts cook beautifully this way. The gravy is excellent

Nancy Coleman
Hartsfield, Georgia

MAMA'S SUNDAY DINNER BEEF ROAST
(A first edition favorite)

3-pound chuck roast
Salt and pepper
Flour
Vegetable oil

Salt and pepper roast. Flour roast on all sides. Put in iron skillet with about 1/2-inch of oil in bottom of skillet. Brown roast on all sides. Place roast in Dutch oven. Add about 4 cups of water to grease left in iron skillet and 3 tablespoons of flour. Bring to a boil. Pour over beef roast and cook in oven at 325 degrees for 2 hours or until tender.

If you came to our house for Sunday dinner, Mama would always have roast beef, rice, macaroni and cheese and banana pudding along with a lot of other goodies. She was a great cook.

Ilene Coleman
Moultrie, Georgia

SUMMER BEEF SALAD

1   (4-5 pound) filet of beef
1   (8-ounce) bottle Italian Salad Dressing
Garlic salt
Seasoned salt
5   sweet red peppers
1   bunch green onions
Mixed salad greens

Several days before serving, marinate beef by pouring salad dressing over filet, then sprinkling generously with garlic salt and seasoned salt. Marinate overnight or at least 12 hours. The day before serving, preheat oven to 400 degrees and cook for 15 minutes; reduce temperature to 350 degrees and cook meat for 15 minutes per pound. Do not over cook. Meat should be medium rare. Cool. Refrigerate for at least 12 hours.

To prepare salad, slice cold beef into thin, bite-size pieces. Seed peppers and slice thinly. Cut roots from onions and chop into small pieces. Combine peppers, onions, and beef. Drizzle with dressing and chill for at least 4 hours. When ready to serve, wash and dry salad greens; loosely tear into pieces. Toss with beef and vegetables to coat with dressing. Yield: 12-16 servings.

Dressing:
1   cup vegetable oil
¾   cup chili sauce
¾   cup red wine vinegar
½   cup sugar
1   tablespoon soy sauce

Combine all ingredients in a jar. Cover tightly and shake vigorously.

Nancy Coleman
Hartsfield, Georgia

Entrees

CHICKEN AND WILD RICE CASSEROLE

1 ½   pounds chicken breasts (bone-in)
¾   pound chicken leg quarters
1   onion, cut in thin slices and separated into rings
¾   teaspoon curry powder
¼   teaspoon black pepper
1   cup cooking sherry
1   (6-ounce) box long grain and wild rice mix (not the kind in pouch)
1   can or jar (6 ounces drained weight) sliced mushrooms
2   (10-¾-ounce) cans cream of mushroom soup
1   cup (8 ounces) sour cream

Place chicken, onion, pepper, curry powder and cooking sherry in a large pot. Add enough water to cover chicken. Heat to boiling, reduce heat. Simmer one hour. Remove chicken, saving broth. Remove chicken from bones. Cut in bite size pieces. Remove onions from broth. Measure broth and use to cook wild rice according to package directions. Set aside. Drain mushrooms. Discard liquid. Combine mushrooms and chopped chicken in a very large container. Stir in rice, mushroom soup, and sour cream. Mix well. Spoon into 13x9-inch baking dish that has been coated with cooking spray. Cover tightly with foil. Refrigerate or freeze until ready to use. Bake the thawed casserole at 350 degrees for 50 minutes. Remove foil. Cover with buttered cracker crumbs and bake 10 additional minutes. Serve hot. Yield: 10 servings

This casserole has been served in the dining room at the Moultrie Federated Guild Antique Show for several years. It is served with a green salad, sour cream muffins and a slice of homemade cake made by Guild members.

Jane G. Gibbs and Virginia T. Hart
Moultrie, Georgia

CHICKEN AND WILD RICE CASSEROLE

(A first edition favorite)

2	cups long grain and wild rice mix
1	cup margarine
½	cup flour
2	(4½-ounce) cans sliced mushrooms
3	cups light cream
1	cup toasted slivered almonds
6	cups cooked and diced chicken
1	cup chopped onions
½	cup pimento
4	tablespoons parsley or 1 teaspoon dried parsley
3	teaspoons salt
½	teaspoon pepper
4	cups chicken broth

Prepare rice according to directions on box. Sauté onions in butter until tender. Remove from heat and stir in flour. Drain mushrooms, reserving the liquid. Combine liquid with enough chicken broth to make 4 cups. Stir slowly into flour mixture. Cook until thickens, stirring constantly. Add rice, mushrooms, chopped chicken, almonds, pimentos, parsley, salt, pepper and cream. Place in large casserole and bake 30 to 40 minutes at 350 degrees. Yield: Serves 20 people.

Will freeze well and is good heated up the next day.

Shirley Tankersley
Ocilla, Georgia

Valued annually at over $745 million, cotton is king of the cash crops in Georgia.

HOT CHICKEN SALAD

1   chicken
Salt, pepper and oregano to taste
2   tablespoons lemon juice
¾   cup mayonnaise
1   teaspoon salt
2   cups celery, finely chopped
2   hard-cooked eggs, chopped
1   (10 ¾-ounce) can cream of chicken soup, undiluted
1   onion, chopped
1   (2-ounce) jar chopped pimiento
1   (4-ounce) can sliced mushrooms (optional)
1½   cups crushed potato chips
1½   cups grated sharp Cheddar cheese
1   cup almonds, toasted and chopped (optional)

Boil chicken with salt, pepper and oregano to taste. Remove chicken from broth (refrigerate broth for use in other recipes), bone and cut into small pieces. Combine all ingredients except potato chips, cheese and almonds. Pour in large greased baking dish. Top with cheese; sprinkle with crushed chips and almonds. Cover and leave in refrigerator overnight or cook at once. Bake at 300 degrees for 20 to 25 minutes. Definitely better when prepared the day before baking making it a good do ahead recipe. Yield: 8-10 servings.

My family doesn't like celery or mushrooms so I leave them out and add 4 additional hard-cooked eggs. I never use the almonds.

Nancy Coleman
Hartsfield, Georgia

RANCH CHICKEN

6	boneless, skinless chicken breasts
1	can cream of chicken soup
1	envelope ranch dressing mix
½	cup water
½	cup sour cream
2	tablespoons ranch dressing
2	tablespoons flour

Spray crock pot with cooking spray. Place chicken breasts in crock pot. In a small bowl, combine soup, dressing mix and water. Pour over chicken and cook on low for 8 hours. Remove chicken. Stir in sour cream, flour and ranch dressing. Replace chicken. Cover and cook on high an additional 20 minutes.

The leftovers are wonderful for sandwiches, wrapped in a tortilla or chicken casserole.

Vivian Morrison
Cusseta, Georgia

ANNIVERSARY CHICKEN

2	tablespoons oil
6	skinless, boneless chicken breasts
½	cup teriyaki basting sauce
½	cup ranch style salad dressing
1	cup shredded Cheddar cheese
3	green onions, chopped
½	can bacon bits
1	tablespoon parsley

Preheat oven to 350 degrees. In a large skillet, heat oil over medium high heat. Add chicken breasts and sauté 4-5 minutes each side, until lightly browned. Place browned chicken breasts in 13x9-inch baking dish. Brush with teriyaki sauce, then spoon on salad dressing. Sprinkle with cheese, green onions, and bacon bits. Bake for 25-35 minutes or until chicken is done. Garnish with parsley.

Mary Walker
Tifton, Georgia

AUSSIE CHICKEN

4   skinless, boneless chicken breasts, pounded to ½ inch thickness
2   teaspoons seasoning salt
6   slices bacon, cut in half
½   cup prepared yellow mustard
½   cup honey
¼   cup light corn syrup
¼   cup mayonnaise
1   tablespoon dried onion flakes
1   tablespoon vegetable oil
2   cups shredded Colby-Monterey Jack cheese
2   tablespoons chopped fresh parsley

Rub the chicken breasts with the seasoning salt, cover and refrigerate for 30 minutes. Preheat oven to 350 degrees. Place bacon in a large, deep skillet. Cook over medium high heat until crisp. Set aside. In a medium bowl, combine the mustard, honey, corn syrup, mayonnaise and dried onion flakes. Remove half of sauce, cover and refrigerate to serve later. Heat oil in a large skillet over medium heat. Place the breasts in the skillet and sauté for 3 to 5 minutes per side, or until browned. Remove from skillet and place the breasts into a 9x13-inch baking dish. Apply the honey mustard sauce to each breast, then layer each breast with bacon. Sprinkle top with shredded cheese. Bake in preheated oven for 35 minutes, or until cheese is melted and chicken juices run clear. Garnish with parsley and serve with the reserved honey mustard sauce.

Lindsey Walker Kaiser
Tifton, Georgia

ILENE'S CHICKEN CASSEROLE
(A first edition favorite)

6 to 8 chicken breast halves
1   **(10 ¾ ounce) can cream of chicken soup**
1   **(10 ¾ ounce) can cream of celery or mushroom soup**
1   **(8 ounce) carton sour cream**
¾   **cup (1½ sticks) margarine, melted**
1   **roll Ritz crackers, crumbled**
Salt to taste

Boil chicken until tender. Cool and cut into small pieces. Add sour cream and soup, mix well. Place in baking dish. Melt margarine; crumble crackers and mix butter and crumbs together. Spread evenly on top of chicken mixture. Bake at 325 degrees until sides bubble and top is golden brown. Yield: 6-8 servings.

Ilene Coleman
Moultrie, Georgia

CRUNCHY ONION CHICKEN

1   **⅓ cup French's French Fried Onions, crumbled**
1   **egg, beaten**
1   **pound boneless, skinless chicken breast**

Put the fried onions in a plastic bag and lightly crush. Dip chicken pieces into eggs then coat with onion crumbs, pressing firmly to adhere to chicken. Place chicken on baking sheet that has been sprayed with cooking spray. Sprinkle on rest of crumbs if needed. Bake at 400 degrees for 20 minutes or until chicken is done in the center.

Linda Stripling
Moultrie, Georgia

CHICKEN TETRAZZINI

1   (8-ounce) package medium egg noodles
1   (4½-ounce) jar sliced mushrooms, liquid reserved
4   tablespoons margarine
3   tablespoons chopped onion
½   teaspoon celery salt
Cayenne pepper, to taste
¼   teaspoon marjoram
1   can cream of chicken soup
1   (12-ounce) can evaporated milk
4   cups chicken, cooked and cubed
2   tablespoons chopped pimiento
½   cup grated sharp Cheddar cheese
¼   cup grated Parmesan cheese

Preheat over to 350 degrees. Cook noodles according to package directions until tender. Drain and rinse with hot water. Drain mushrooms, reserving liquid. Melt margarine in large pan. Sauté onions. Reduce heat; add seasonings and mushroom liquid. Blend in soup and stir until smooth. Gradually add evaporated milk. Stir until smooth and thickened. Add chicken, mushrooms and pimiento to sauce. Combine with noodles, mixing well. Place chicken and noodle mixture in baking dish which has been treated with cooking spray. Top with Cheddar cheese and Parmesan cheese. Bake for 30 minutes or until bubbly. Yield: 8-10 servings

One of the mothers prepared this for a youth group supper at the church. To my surprise, the youth loved it.

Nancy Coleman
Hartsfield, Georgia

164

POTATO CHIP CHICKEN TENDERS

8-10 boneless chicken tenders
2   cups crushed potato chips
2   eggs, beaten
2   tablespoons water
Ground black pepper

Beat eggs and water together in a small bowl. Place potato chips in a separate small bowl. Dip chicken tenders in eggs, roll in potato chips. Place on baking sheet. Spray chicken with cooking spray. Sprinkle fresh ground pepper over all chicken pieces. Bake at 350 degrees for 15-20 minutes or until juices run clear.

Norma Crawford Thomas
Bishop, Georgia

MOTHER'S CHICKEN AND DRESSING

1   chicken, cooked, boned and cut into pieces
Chicken broth (from chicken)
1   (9x13-inch) pan cooked homemade cornbread
3   slices white sandwich bread
2   cans cream of chicken soup
2   cans chicken broth
4   eggs, beaten
1   teaspoon poultry seasoning
1   medium onion, chopped
4   stalks celery, chopped
1   stick butter or margarine
Salt and pepper

Mix together cornbread, white bread, chicken broths, soups, eggs, lots of salt and pepper, and poultry seasoning. Sauté onions and celery in butter. Add to bread mixture. Add cut-up chicken pieces. Mix together and bake at 350 degrees for about 40 minutes. Be careful not to overcook.

My mother, Edith Stripling, made this dressing every Thanksgiving and Christmas for her family. She loved to cook. My prayer is that her art will not be lost in generations to come.

Charlotte Mathis
Moultrie, Georgia

FIX AHEAD CHICKEN CASSEROLE

2	cups chopped cooked chicken breasts
½	pound Velveeta cheese
1	can cream of mushroom soup
1	can cream of chicken soup
1½	cups water
1	(8-ounce) package shell macaroni, uncooked
3	hard-cooked eggs, chopped
1	small jar diced pimientos

Mix all ingredients together and put in refrigerator overnight. Bake 350 degrees for 30 minutes.

Brenda Morris
Ocilla, Georgia

RUSSIAN CHICKEN

	6 to 8 chicken breasts or pieces
1	(8-ounce) bottle Russian dressing
1	(8-ounce) jar apricot preserves
1	envelope onion soup mix
¼	cup water
1	pineapple slice for each piece of chicken, optional

Place chicken in baking dish. Mix remaining ingredients except pineapple and pour over chicken. Cover with foil. Bake at 350 degrees for 1 hour. Uncover and place pineapple on chicken. Cook 30 minutes more uncovered.

Jane Gibbs
Moultrie, Georgia

Entrees

CHICKEN SPECTACULAR

3	cups cooked chicken, chopped
1	(14.5-ounce) can green string beans, undrained
1	box Rice-a-Roni, chicken flavor, prepared to directions
1	can cream of celery soup
½	cup mayonnaise
1	small can sliced water chestnuts
½	cup chopped onions
2	tablespoons chopped pimiento
Salt and pepper to taste	
1	small package slivered almonds

Using a large mixing bowl, mix all ingredients, except the slivered almonds, until well mixed. Spray a 9 x13-inch casserole dish with cooking spray. Scatter the slivered almonds on top. Bake at 350 degrees for approximately 30 minutes.

Linda Stripling
Moultrie, Georgia

CHICKEN PIE

6-7	chicken thighs, cooked and chopped
2	cups chicken broth
1	can cream of celery soup
7	hard-cooked eggs, sliced
¼	cup margarine, melted
1	cup self-rising flour
1	cup buttermilk
1	small can peas and carrots mixed, drained
Salt and pepper to taste	

Put chicken in bottom of casserole dish. Cover with peas and carrots. Mix soup and broth together and pour over pie. Mix margarine, flour and buttermilk together and pour over pie. Cook at 400 degrees for 45 minutes to 1 hour.

Myra Kirksey
Byromville, Georgia

Entrees

CHICKEN CASSEROLE

1	frying chicken, boiled and boned
½	cup chopped onion, cooked
1	package Herb Rice-a-Roni
¾	cup broth from cooked chicken
1	(4-ounce) jar chopped pimiento
¼	cup butter, melted
1	can cream of mushroom soup
1	teaspoon parsley flakes
1 ¼	cups evaporated milk

Cook Rice-a-Roni according to package, using stock from cooked chicken. Mix all ingredients well. Put in 9x13-inch baking dish and cook at 375 degrees about 30-45 minutes. If it is not as brown on top as you would like it turn on broiler for a minute and brown.

Mary Walker
Tifton, Georgia

Each acre of cotton yields over 1100 pounds of seed and only about 840 pounds of fiber.

Entrees

SPINACH-CHICKEN LASAGNA

6	lasagna noodles, cooked
1	(10-ounce) package frozen spinach, thawed
2	cups cooked chicken
2	cups grated Cheddar cheese
⅓	cup onion, chopped
1	tablespoon cornstarch
½	teaspoon salt
¼	teaspoon pepper
1	tablespoon soy sauce
1	can cream of mushroom soup
8	ounces sour cream
1	jar (4.5 ounces) mushrooms, drained
⅓	cup mayonnaise
1	cup fresh Parmesan cheese
2	tablespoons butter, melted
1	cup pecans, chopped

Combine spinach, chicken, cheese, onion, cornstarch, salt, pepper, soy sauce, mushroom soup, sour cream, mushrooms and mayonnaise. Alternate noodles and chicken mixture. Sprinkle with Parmesan cheese. Mix butter and pecans and sprinkle on top. Bake at 350 degrees for 55-60 minutes.

Brenda Morris
Ocilla, Georgia

EASY ITALIAN CHICKEN

4	boneless, skinless chicken breasts
Salt and pepper	
1	(24-ounce) jar marinara sauce
1	cup grated Italian blend cheese or Mozzarella cheese

Season chicken breasts as desired. Cook in skillet in small amount of olive oil until done. Place in greased casserole dish. Add marinara sauce to pan to deglaze. Pour sauce over chicken and top with cheese. Bake at 350 degrees until cheese is melted. Serve with prepared angel hair pasta. Yield: 4 servings

Nancy Coleman
Hartsfield, Georgia

CHICKEN PARMESAN

4   boneless, skinless chicken breasts
1   egg
½   cup milk
Italian bread crumbs
1   (16-ounce) jar spaghetti sauce
2   cups grated Mozzarella cheese
Parmesan cheese
Olive oil

Whisk together egg and milk. Flatten chicken breasts until uniform thickness. Dip chicken breasts in milk and egg mixture. Dredge in bread crumbs. Pour a small amount of olive oil in skillet over medium heat. Brown chicken breasts on both sides until golden brown. Place chicken in greased casserole dish. Pour spaghetti sauce over chicken. Sprinkle cheese over sauce. Bake at 350 degrees 25-30 minutes until bubbly. Serve with cooked spaghetti noodles. Yield: 4 servings.

Nancy Coleman
Hartsfield, Georgia

MOZZARELLA CHICKEN

6   chicken breasts (or strips)
1   can chicken broth
1   egg
Italian bread crumbs
1   stick butter
2   cups Mozzarella cheese, grated

Marinate chicken in egg for 1 hour (I have just rolled in egg). Roll in bread crumbs. Melt butter in fry pan. Brown chicken lightly (just until brown). Place in casserole dish. Pour chicken broth over chicken. Top with cheese. Cover and bake at 375 degrees for 40 minutes. Remove cover and continue baking 15-20 minutes or until brown.

This is a recipe I found in ABAC cookbook that was from Brenda Clark Chandler (Nancy Coleman's sister). It is one of our favorites.

Yvonne H. Crawford
Chula, Georgia

Entrees

CHICKEN SPAGHETTI

1   hen
1   onion, chopped
1   (16-ounce) package spaghetti
1   cup diced celery
2   (14.5-ounce) cans tomatoes
1   (15-ounce) can English peas
2   cups grated Cheddar cheese
Pepper and paprika

Boil hen in large pot until tender (be sure to spray pot with cooking spray). Remove chicken from broth, bone and chop chicken. Skim fat from broth and put in skillet. Sauté onion and celery in fat until tender but not brown. Cook spaghetti in broth. Add peas and tomatoes (do not drain) to onions and celery. Simmer while spaghetti is cooking. When spaghetti is done, return vegetables and chicken to pot. Add noodles. Simmer 15 to 20 minutes stirring occasionally. Add grated cheese. Allow cheese to melt. (Mixture will scorch easily after cheese is added.) Simmer for a few minutes.

This is great for a crowd. If there is any left over, it's just as good warmed over as it was the first time. It also freezes well.

Lois Clark
Cairo, Georgia

TACO CHICKEN

Whole chicken, boiled and skinned
1   onion, chopped
1   (8-ounce) can cream of mushroom soup
1   cup milk
1   package taco seasoning mix
2   cups shredded cheese
Tortilla chips

Chop chicken and mix with onion, cream of mushroom soup, milk, taco seasoning mix, 1 cup shredded cheese. Line a 7x11-inch dish with tortilla chips overlapping and standing up the sides. Pour chicken mixture over chips and cover with remaining cup of cheese. Bake at 350 degrees 20 minutes or until heated.

Mary Walker
Tifton, Georgia

SALSA CHICKEN

4   skinless, boneless chicken breasts
1   cup shredded Cheddar cheese
4   teaspoons taco seasoning mix
2   tablespoons sour cream
1   cup salsa

Preheat oven to 375 degrees. Place chicken in lightly greased baking dish. Sprinkle taco seasoning on both sides of chicken breasts, and pour salsa over all. Bake for 25-35 minutes or until chicken is done. Sprinkle evenly with cheese and continue baking for an additional 3-5 minutes or until cheese is melted and bubbly. Serves 4.

Mary Walker
Tifton, Georgia

MEXICAN CHICKEN

2   whole chicken breasts
1   can Rotel tomatoes and chilies
1   cup chicken broth
1   (8-ounce) package taco-flavored Doritos
1   can cream of mushroom soup
1   onion, chopped
1   can cream of chicken
1 ½   cups shredded cheese

Boil chicken, bone, and cut up into bite size pieces. Line 2-quart shallow, greased casserole with slightly crushed Doritos. Put chicken and chopped onion of top. Mix rest of ingredients (except cheese) and pour over chicken and Doritos. Top with shredded cheese. Bake at 350 degrees for 30 minutes.

Mary Walker
Tifton, Georgia

MEXICAN CHICKEN BAKE

1   medium onion, chopped
1   small green pepper, seeded and chopped
2   large jalapeño peppers, seeded and chopped
¼   cup butter or margarine
2   (10 ¾ ounce) cans cream of chicken soup
1   (12-ounce) can evaporated milk
4   cups cooked long-grain rice
3 to 4 cups cubed, cooked chicken
3   cups (12 ounces) Colby-Monterey Jack cheese

Sauté onion, green pepper and jalapeño peppers in butter until tender. In a bowl, combine soup and milk. Stir in the rice, chicken and 2 cups of cheese and onion/pepper mixture. Transfer to a greased 13x9-inch baking dish. Bake uncovered at 350 degrees for 25 minutes. Sprinkle with the remaining cheese. Bake 5-10 minutes longer or until heated through and cheese is melted.

For the chicken, I boil 4 chicken breasts.

Reba Ledden Milliron
Shellman, Georgia

"Wrinkle-free" cotton, which has a resin finish to prevent wrinkling, has served to further increase the demand for cotton in corporate casual apparel.

FIESTA PIE

3   eggs
¾   cup milk
2   cups chicken flavor or cornbread stuffing mix
1½   cups cubed, cooked chicken
1   large tomato, chopped
3   tablespoons chopped green onions
3   tablespoons chopped green chilies
Salsa
Sour cream

Beat eggs in a large bowl; stir in milk. Add remaining ingredients except salsa and sour cream; mix well. Pour mixture into greased 9-inch microwavable pie plate. Cover loosely with wax paper. Microwave on high 5 minutes. Stir edges of mixture into center and from center to outside edges, smoothing out surface. Cover. Microwave 4 minutes or until center is no longer wet. Remove from microwave oven. Let stand 5 minutes. Serve immediately with salsa and sour cream. Yield: 6 servings.

Mary Walker
Tifton, Georgia

When seeding jalapeño peppers, use rubber or plastic gloves and wash your hands immediately with soapy water when finished. The seeds and membranes are very hot and can burn your hands. Do not touch your eyes, nose or mouth before washing hands.

Entrees

CHICKEN ENCHILADAS

5	chicken breasts
1	medium onion
2	(8-ounce) packages cream cheese
2	cups milk

Grated sharp Cheddar cheese

Tortillas

Cook chicken; cut into bite size pieces. Dice onion and sauté in butter. Mix chicken, onion and cream cheese in saucepan, melting cream cheese and blending ingredients. Put about ½ cup of the meat mixture on the tortilla shell, rollup tortilla and place in a 9x13-inch casserole that has been coated with cooking spray. Continue until all meat mixture is used, placing tortillas side by side in the casserole dish. Top with milk and sprinkle the cheese on top. Bake at 350 degrees (about 30-40 minutes) until bubbly and cheese has melted.

Wonderful. Children and teenagers love it!

Gail Thompson
Moultrie, Georgia

CREAMY CHICKEN ENCHILADAS

1	tablespoon butter
1	onion, chopped
1	(4-ounce) can chopped green chilies
1	(8-ounce) package cream cheese
3 ½	cups chopped, cooked chicken
8	(8 ½ -inch) flour tortillas
16	ounces Monterey Jack cheese, shredded
2	cups heavy cream

Heat butter in large skillet over medium heat. Sauté onion in butter for 5 minutes. Add the green chilies, stir 1 minute. Stir in the cream cheese and chicken. Cook until cream cheese is melted. Place a spoonful of the chicken mixture down the center of each tortilla. Roll up tortilla and place seam side down in a lightly greased 9x13-inch baking dish. Sprinkle with cheese and drizzle with the cream. Bake at 350 degrees or until bubbly. Yield: 8 servings.

Helen Sewell,
Moultrie, Georgia

CILANTRO-LIME CHICKEN

1	bunch fresh cilantro
⅓	cup lime juice
¼	cup olive oil
6	boned and skinned chicken breasts
1	teaspoon minced ginger
2	teaspoon minced garlic

Reserve some sprigs of cilantro for garnish, chop remainder. Combine the chopped cilantro, lime juice, and olive oil in a measuring cup. Pour about ½ of the mixture into a shallow dish. Reserve remaining marinade to use on the cooked chicken. Pat the chicken breasts dry with paper towel and dredge them in marinade (discard any marinade that remains in dish). Season the chicken with salt and pepper and grill until thoroughly cooked, about 6 minutes on each side. Add 1 teaspoon minced ginger and 2 teaspoons minced garlic to the reserved marinade and drizzle on the grilled chicken.

Lindsey Walker Kaiser
Tifton, Georgia

176

Entrees

SANTA FE CHICKEN

(A first edition favorite)

6   boneless, skinless chicken breasts
Lowry's Seasoning Salt
1   green bell pepper, sliced
1   red bell pepper, sliced
1   yellow bell pepper, sliced
1   onion, sliced
1   can fully seasoned black beans, drained
1   (16-ounce) jar salsa
Freshly chopped cilantro
6   servings yellow or Spanish rice, cooked
Monterey Jack cheese, grated (optional)

Sprinkle chicken with seasoning salt. Cook chicken breasts until done in skillet with as little oil as possible oil (you may also grill or bake). When done, remove from skillet and place in a large baking dish. Sauté peppers and onions until tender. Pour black beans over chicken; top with sautéed peppers and onions. Pour salsa over top of peppers. Sprinkle cilantro and cheese on top. Bake at 350 degrees until hot throughout and cheese has melted. To serve, spoon rice on to serving plate and top with chicken. Yield: 6 servings.

A zesty and colorful dish.

Nancy Coleman
Hartsfield, Georgia

EASY MEXICAN CHICKEN

4   boneless, skinless chicken breasts
Salt and pepper
1   (16 ounce) jar salsa
1   cup grated Mexican blend cheese

Season chicken breasts as desired. Cook in skillet in small amount of oil until done. (May also be grilled.) Place in greased casserole dish. Add salsa to pan to deglaze. Pour salsa over chicken and top with cheese. Bake at 350 degrees until cheese is melted. Serve with yellow or Spanish rice. Yield: 4 servings

Nancy Coleman
Hartsfield, Georgia

CHICKEN WITH PINEAPPLE SAUCE

2	tablespoons brown sugar
1	tablespoon cornstarch
2	(8-ounce) cans crushed pineapple, undrained
¼	cup soy sauce
¼	teaspoon garlic salt
¼	teaspoon ground ginger
6	boneless, skinless chicken breasts

In a saucepan, combine brown sugar and cornstarch. Stir in pineapple, soy sauce, garlic salt and ginger. Bring to a boil; cook and stir for 2 minutes until thickened. Place chicken in a greased 9- inch square baking dish. Pour half the sauce over chicken. Bake, uncovered, for 15 minutes in a preheated 350-degree oven; baste. Bake 10 minutes longer or until chicken juices run clear, basting several times with remaining sauce. Excellent served with rice, especially jasmine rice. Yield: 6 servings.

Nancy Coleman
Hartsfield, Georgia

GRILLED HAWAIIAN CHICKEN

4	boneless, skinless chicken breasts
¼	cup soy sauce
½	cup Worcestershire sauce
1	small can sliced pineapple, drain and reserve juice

Combine soy sauce, Worcestershire sauce and reserved pineapple juice. Marinate chicken breasts in mixture for about 1 hour. Grill breasts. When done, grill pineapple slices and top chicken breasts.

Nancy Coleman
Hartsfield, Georgia

TERIYAKI CHICKEN

| 18 | bamboo skewers |
| 24 | chicken thighs, bones removed |

Teriyaki Sauce:

2	tablespoons cornstarch
2	tablespoons cold water
1	cup sugar
1	cup soy sauce
½	cup apple cider vinegar
2	cloves garlic, minced
1	teaspoon ground ginger
	Black pepper to taste

Mix all sauce ingredients in a small saucepan. Bring to a boil, stirring frequently, and remove from the heat. Preheat oven to 425 degrees. Soak bamboo skewers in water for 20 minutes. Remove excess fat from chicken thighs and cut into large bite-size pieces. Thread chicken onto skewers. Line a relatively deep pan with aluminum foil. Spread part of the sauce on the bottom of the pan. Place each kabob on the teriyaki sauce, turning so all sides get coated with the sauce. Bake for 40 minutes. Yield: 18 servings

If you don't have skewers, just put the chicken in the pan and coat with sauce. I use chicken tenders instead of thighs.

Nancy Coleman
Hartsfield, Georgia

FRUITED CHICKEN SALAD

4	cups chopped, cooked chicken
2	cups diced celery
2	cups halved seedless red or green grapes
1	(15.25-ounce) can pineapple tidbits, drained
1	(11-ounce) can Mandarin oranges, drained
1	cup slivered almonds, toasted
½	cup mayonnaise
½	cup sour cream
2	tablespoons lemon juice
¼	teaspoon salt
¼	teaspoon white pepper

Fresh escarole

Combine chicken, celery, grapes, pineapple, oranges and almond and toss well. Combine mayonnaise, sour cream, lemon juice, salt and white pepper; add to chicken mixture, stirring well. Chill. Serve on bed of escarole. Yield: 24 servings, ½ cup each

Virginia Hart
Moultrie, Georgia

Sprinkle apple or pear slices with lemon juice as soon as you slice them to prevent browning. If you're out of lemon juice, use a diet lemon-lime soft drink. It won't affect the taste of the fruit.

Entrees

SEVEN LAYER CHINESE CHICKEN SALAD

5	cups Romaine lettuce
1	package chicken-flavor Ramen noodles with soup mix, uncooked
2	cups diced, cooked chicken
1	can white corn
1 ½	tomatoes, diced
½-1	cup green onions (optional)
1	cup lightly salted peanuts

Crush the noodles and use uncooked. Layer above ingredients in a bowl.

Dressing:

2	tablespoons sugar
1	teaspoon salt
¾	teaspoon grated ginger
½	teaspoon pepper
¼	cup oil, vegetable or olive
3	tablespoons vinegar
	Seasoning packet from Ramen noodles

Mix the dressing ingredients and pour dressing over layered salad and enjoy!

Julie Evans Crawford
Oviedo, Florida

TURKEY OSSO BUCCO

½   breast of turkey (cut into 3 pieces, preferably by the butcher)
2   turkey thighs
Salt and freshly ground black pepper
⅓   cup all-purpose flour, for dredging
½   cup vegetable oil
1   small onion, finely diced
1   carrot, finely diced
1   celery stalk, finely diced
1   tablespoon tomato paste
1   cup dry white wine
4   cups reduce-sodium chicken broth
1   large sprig fresh rosemary
2   large sprigs fresh thyme
2   bay leaves
2   whole cloves

Preheat the oven to 375 degrees F. Pat the turkey with paper towels to dry and ensure even browning. Season the turkey with salt and pepper. Dredge the turkey in the flour to coat. In a heavy roasting pan large enough to fit the turkey in a single layer, heat the oil over medium heat. Add the turkey and cook until brown on both sides, about 6 minutes per side. Transfer the turkey to a plate and reserve. In the same pan, add the onion, carrot, and celery. Season vegetables with salt. Cook until the vegetables are tender, about 6 minutes. Stir in the tomato paste and cook for 1 minute. Stir in the wine and simmer until the Turkey Osso Buco with Parsley and Rosemary Gremolata liquid is reduced by half, about 3 minutes. Return the turkey to the pan. Add enough chicken broth to come ⅔ up the sides of the turkey. Add the herb sprigs, bay leaf, and cloves to the broth mixture. Bring the liquid to a boil over medium-high heat. Remove the pan from the heat. Cover the pan tightly with foil and transfer to the oven. Braise until the turkey is fork-tender, turning the turkey after 1 hour.

TURKEY OSSO BUCCO, continued

Gremolata:
The gremolata is the perfect finish and the whole dish looks beautiful on the platter.

    ¼   cup chopped fresh flat-leaf parsley
    Zest of 1 lemon
    2   cloves garlic, minced
    1   teaspoon minced rosemary leaves
    Pinch salt
    Pinch freshly ground black pepper

Combine the chopped parsley, lemon zest, garlic, minced rosemary, and a pinch of salt and freshly ground black pepper in a bowl. Cover and reserve until serving the turkey.

To serve, transfer the turkey to shallow serving bowl. Season the sauce to taste with salt and pepper. Ladle the sauce over the meat. Sprinkle each piece of turkey with a large pinch of Gremolata. Serve immediately. Yield: 4 to 6 servings

Traditional Osso Bucco is made with veal shank which is also delicious but quite expensive. If using veal shank, preparation is the same. Wine is key in this dish and you should use one suitable for drinking. More broth can be substituted in place of the wine, if preferred.

Karen Nikitopoulos
Georgia Cotton Commission
Perry, Georgia

TURKEY POT PIE

1 ½	cups cooked Jennie-O Turkey Roast, cubed
¼	cup butter
⅓	cup flour
⅓	cup chopped onion
¾	teaspoon salt
⅓	teaspoon pepper
1 ½	cups chicken broth
½	cup milk
2	cups mixed vegetables
¼	cup Jennie-O turkey gravy (optional)
15	ounce package refrigerated pie crust

Heat oven to 425 degrees. Place one pie crust in 9-inch pie pan according to package directions. In medium saucepan, melt butter over medium heat. Add onions; cook until tender, about 2 minutes. Stir in flour, salt and pepper. Cook stirring constantly, until mixture is bubbly, remove from heat. Stir in broth and milk. Heat to boiling, stirring constantly. Boil and stir 1 minute. Stir in turkey, and vegetables, remove from heat. Spoon turkey filling over crust. Place second crust over filling; flute edge. Cut slits in several places. Bake for 35 to 40 minutes or until crust is golden brown.

Vickie Abrams
Berlin, Georgia

FRIED TURKEY

(A first edition favorite)

1   onion
1   bell pepper
Turkey

Season mix:
4   tablespoons salt
1   tablespoon black pepper
1   teaspoon red pepper
1   teaspoon onion powder
1   teaspoon garlic powder

Put onion and bell pepper in blender; blend till liquid. Add enough water if needed to make 2 cups of liquid. To liquid add 1 teaspoon of season mix. Inject turkey every 2 inches all over. Refrigerate at least 12 hours, better if it marinates 24 hours. Have enough cooking oil or grease (hog lard works best in the opinion of person who gave me this recipe, but not me) to cover turkey, bring temperature to 350 degrees. Cook at 350 degrees for 3 minutes per pound plus 3 minutes.

This recipe belongs to our first Fire Chief, Rev. Jack Thompson. He is not only a good preacher and a first class fire chief, but a real good cook.

Mary Register
Waterloo, Georgia

RIBS WITH DRY RUB

Rub:

1	teaspoon ground black pepper
1	teaspoon ground white pepper
2	teaspoons sugar
2	teaspoons cayenne pepper
2	teaspoons chili powder
1	teaspoon cumin
1	teaspoon garlic powder
6	teaspoons light brown sugar
2	teaspoons ground oregano
2	teaspoons paprika
1	teaspoon dry mustard
2	teaspoons celery salt
1	teaspoon salt

1	rack of ribs

Prepared mustard

Preparation: Mix rub ingredients together. Remove thin membrane from inside of ribs, trim excess fat, wash, and dry with paper towels. Brush dry ribs with liquid mustard (plain sandwich mustard). Use only enough to make a very thin sticky surface on the ribs to allow the spices to stick to the ribs. Allow to dry for a few minutes. Sprinkle ribs with rub mixture and gently massage into meat on both sides. Wrap tightly in plastic wrap and store overnight or at least 8 hours in refrigerator.

Cooking: Cook for approximately 3-4 hours over indirect heat at 200-225 degrees. Turn ribs about every 30 minutes to ensure even cooking and no burning. If desired gently brush with your favorite BBQ sauce at last turning. Any sooner and sauce will form a crust.

Clint Abrams
Berlin, Georgia

Entrees

PORK CHOP CASSEROLE

(A first edition favorite)

4	pork chops
	Salt and pepper
1	cup uncooked rice
2	onions, chopped
2	(10.5-ounce) cans beef consommé
1	(4-ounce) can sliced mushrooms, drained (optional)
¼	cup (½ stick) butter or margarine

Season pork chops. In a skillet, brown pork chops in butter. Put pork chops in casserole dish coated with cooking spray. Sauté onion in butter. Mix remaining ingredients, cooking long enough to deglaze skillet. Pour over pork chops. Cover with foil or lid. Bake 1 hour at 350 degrees. Yield: 4 servings.

One of our favorite recipes. One day I didn't have any consommé so I used a package of onion soup mix and two cups of water. Equally as good.

Nancy Coleman
Hartsfield, Georgia

SLOW-COOKER BAKED HAM

2	cups brown sugar
1	(8-pound) cured, bone in picnic ham

Spread 1½ cups brown sugar in the bottom of a slow cooker or crock-pot. Place the ham flat side down in the slow cooker. (You may trim some fat to make it fit in the cooker.) Use hands to rub the remaining brown sugar into the ham. Cover and cook on low for 8 hours.

Linda Stripling
Moultrie, Georgia

BAKED PORK TENDERLOIN
WITH MUSTARD SAUCE

2 ½   to 3 pound fresh pork tenderloin
1   (12-ounce) bottle Lawry's Teriyaki with pineapple juice
       marinade

Place the pork tenderloin in large zip-lock bag and pour in marinade. Marinate
for several hours. Remove from marinade and bake at 325 degrees basting
frequently (with marinade) for about 1 hour or until tender. Carve into thin
diagonal slices and serve with mustard sauce. Yield: 8 servings

Mustard Sauce:
⅓   cup sour cream
⅓   cup mayonnaise
1   tablespoon dry mustard
1   tablespoon finely chopped scallions
1½   teaspoon vinegar
½   teaspoon salt

Mix together and stir until smooth.

*My son-in-law, Steve Tyus, cooks the meat on the smoker also — and it is
delicious!*

Charlotte Mathis
Moultrie, Georgia

188

Entrees

ROAST PORK LOIN
WITH PLUM SAUCE

5-8 pound pork loin
Garlic salt
Onion salt
Pepper

Preheat oven to 325 degrees. Rub spices into pork. Place pork roast on rack in shallow roasting pan. Do not add water. Do not cover. Roast until meat thermometer inserted in thickest part of roast registers 155-160 degrees. Allow 23-30 minutes per pound.

Plum Sauce:

2	tablespoons butter
¾	cup chopped onion
1	cup red plum preserves
½	cup brown sugar, packed
⅔	cup water
2	tablespoons lemon juice
⅓	cup chili sauce
¼	cup soy sauce
2	teaspoons prepared mustard
3	drops Tabasco sauce

Melt butter in skillet and sauté onion until tender. Add remaining ingredients; simmer 15 minutes. Pour fat off pork, pour half of sauce over meat. Bake 20-30 minutes longer, basting often. Serve extra sauce on side. Serves 6

Sauce is delicious with any cut of pork.

Nancy Coleman
Hartsfield, Georgia

PRALINE PORK CHOPS

6	boneless pork chops
2	teaspoons Creole seasoning
¼	cup butter, melted
1	tablespoon vegetable oil
1 ⅓	cup maple syrup
½	cup brown sugar
1	cup chopped pecans, toasted

Sprinkle both sides of pork chops with Creole seasoning. Heat butter and oil in large skillet on medium-high heat until hot. Add pork chops and cook 4 to 5 minutes on each side until done. Remove meat, reserving drippings in skillet. Place pork chops on serving platter; set aside and keep warm. Add maple syrup and sugar to drippings in skillet; bring to boil. Stir in pecans, and cook 1 minute until thoroughly heated. Spoon pecan mixture over pork chops. Yield: 6 servings

Oh, so good and oh, so Southern. Boneless, skinless chicken breasts can be substituted for the pork chops.

Nancy Coleman
Hartsfield, Georgia

SAUSAGE EGG BAKE

1	pound sausage
2	cans cream of potato soup
9	eggs
⅓	cup milk
¼	teaspoon black pepper
4	ounces shredded Cheddar cheese

Cook sausage over medium heat in a skillet until no longer pink; drain. Stir in soup. In a mixing bowl, beat eggs, milk and pepper; stir in sausage mixture. Transfer to a lightly greased 11x7-inch dish. Sprinkle with cheese. Bake uncovered at 375 degrees for 40-45 minutes. Yield: 12 servings.

Myra Kirksey
Byromville, Georgia

CRESCENT BREAKFAST BAKE

2   packages refrigerated crescent dinner rolls
1   pound sausage
1   (8-ounce) package cream cheese

Brown and drain sausage. Soften cream cheese. Open crescent rolls, unroll and line 9x13-inch baking dish with one package of crescent rolls. Mix sausage and cream cheese together. Spread over rolls (bottom crust). Place the other package of rolls on top of sausage mixture. Seal edges of rolls as well as you can. Bake 350 degrees for 30 minutes or until brown. Yield: 6 servings.

Patsy Wester
Meigs, Georgia

HASH BROWN BREAKFAST CASSEROLE

1   pound hot bulk pork sausage
3   cups hash brown potatoes, thawed
½   teaspoon salt
3   cups shredded Cheddar cheese
½   cup chopped green bell pepper (optional)
½   cup chopped onion (optional)
12   eggs, beaten
2   cups milk

Brown the sausage (with onion if desired) in a skillet, stirring until crumbly; drain well. Place the potatoes in a lightly greased 9x13-inch baking dish. Sprinkle with salt. Layer the sausage, cheese and green peppers over the potatoes. Combine the eggs and milk in a bowl and mix well. Pour over the green peppers. Cover and refrigerate overnight. Bake at 350 degrees for 50 minutes. Yield: 10 servings.

Mary B. Smith
Brinson, Georgia

Entrees

SAUSAGE JAMBALAYA

(A favorite from the first edition)

1	tablespoon canola oil
1	large onion, chopped
1	pound spicy sausage, cut diagonally into ½" slices
3	large bell peppers, seeded and cut into chunks
2	celery stalks, chopped
1	garlic clove, minced
1	teaspoon cayenne pepper
½	teaspoon paprika
1	pound fresh or frozen okra, cut into small pieces
1	cup long-grain rice
3	cups chicken broth
1	bay leaf

In a large nonstick skillet over medium-high heat, heat oil. Add the sausage and sauté about 5 minutes until sausage is lightly browned. Remove to paper towels to drain. To skillet, add onion, bell peppers, celery, and garlic; sauté about 5 minutes until vegetables are soft. Stir in the cayenne and paprika, and cook 1 minute. Return the sausage to skillet with okra, rice, broth and bay leaf. Bring to a boil; then reduce heat, cover and simmer about 25 minutes or until the rice is tender and liquid has been absorbed. Remove bay leaf and let stand 5 or 10 minutes before serving.

Charlotte Wingate
Doerun, Georgia

SHRIMP AND GRITS

1	pound large raw shrimp, peeled and deveined*
1	cup heavy cream
2	cups water
1½	cups hot stock (shrimp, chicken, or vegetable)
¼	cup butter

Salt and black pepper to taste

1	cup stone-ground grits (do not use quick grits)
3	tablespoons fresh lemon juice

Salt and black pepper to taste

6	bacon slices
2	tablespoons finely chopped onion
1	clove garlic, minced
2	tablespoons finely chopped green or red bell pepper

*To make shrimp stock, place the shells of the shrimp in a saucepan and cover with water. Simmer over low heat approximately 7 to 10 minutes. Remove from heat and strain the broth, discarding shells. Add shrimp broth to hot stock to yield 1 ½ cups.

In a large saucepan over medium-high heat, combine cream, water, and hot stock; bring to a gentle boil. Add butter, salt, and pepper. Slowly add grits, stirring constantly (so that the grits do not settle to the bottom and scorch), until all are added; reduce heat to medium-low. Cook for 20 minutes, stirring occasionally (be careful not to scorch mixture), or until the grits are tender. Grits should have absorbed all of the liquid and become soft and should have the same consistency as oatmeal (moist, not dry). If the grits become too thick, add warm stock or water to thin. Remove from heat.

Sprinkle shrimp with lemon juice, salt, and pepper; set aside. In a large frying pan over medium-high heat, cook bacon until brown but not crisp. Remove from heat and pat dry with paper towels; set aside. Coarsely chop bacon when cool. Reserve 4 tablespoons bacon grease in the frying pan. Add onion, garlic, and green or red bell pepper; sauté 10 minutes or until the onion is transparent. Add shrimp mixture and bacon; sauté 5 to 7 minutes or until shrimp are opaque in center (cut to test). Remove from heat. To serve, spoon hot grits onto individual serving plates and top with shrimp mixture. Yield: 4 servings.

Nancy Coleman
Hartsfield, Georgia

BILOXI SHRIMP SALAD

(A first edition favorite)

5	pounds boiled shrimp
6	chopped bell peppers
1	bunch chopped green onions (with tops)

Salt and pepper to taste

1	pint mayonnaise
2	cups chopped celery
2	dozen hard-cooked eggs
1	(8 ounce) jar sweet relish

Mix the chopped onions, peppers, sweet relish, celery and the yellow of the eggs with the mayonnaise, saving three or four eggs for garnish. Chop the shrimp and whites of the eggs and add to the mixture. Serve on lettuce leaves garnished with slices of the remaining eggs and sprinkle with chopped parsley.

Charlotte Wingate
Doerun, Georgia

CRUSTLESS CRAB QUICHE

½	pound fresh mushrooms
2	tablespoons butter
4	eggs
1	cup sour cream
1	cup cottage cheese
1	cup Parmesan cheese
4	tablespoons flour
1	teaspoon onion powder
¼	teaspoon salt
1	teaspoon Dijon mustard
½	pound shredded Monterey Jack Cheese
2	cans crabmeat, drained

Sauté mushrooms in butter and drain. Place sautéed mushrooms, Monterey Jack cheese and crabmeat in greased quiche dish. Blend other ingredients and pour over crabmeat mixture and bake at 350 degrees for 45 minutes.

Maurissa Smith
Atlanta, Georgia

SLOW-COOKED CUBED DEER

1   (8-ounce) can of cream of mushroom soup
1   (8-ounce) can of beef consommé
1   cup water
Cubed deer steak
Flour
Salt and pepper

Mix cream of mushroom soup, beef consommé and water. Flour and season cubed deer steak (cubed beef steak can be substituted). Lightly brown steak on both sides. Place steak in slow cooker and cover with the mixed ingredients. Cook for 8 hours on low in a slow cooker.

This is great to serve over rice and serve hot rolls.

Teresa Cromer Walker
Tifton, GA

HOT CHICKEN SALAD

2 cups chicken, chopped
2 cups celery, chopped
3 tablespoons minced onion
3 tablespoons lemon juice
½ teaspoon salt
¾ cup mayonnaise
1 small can mushrooms, optional
1 can cream of chicken soup
2 cups shredded cheese
Crushed potato chips, garnish

Mix chicken, celery, onion, lemon juice, salt, mayonnaise and mushrooms. Pour into casserole dish and spread soup on top without stirring. Add cheese and chips on top of soup and bake at 300 degrees for 35 minutes.

Kim Miller Thompson
Dalton, Georgia

CLEMONS CHICKEN

8   chicken breasts
2   celery stalks
4   sprigs parsley
1   carrot
1   onion
Salt and pepper to taste

Cook chicken and vegetables together in water. Strain broth, take chicken out and mix together as directed below:

6   tablespoons minced onion
1   cup butter
8   tablespoons all-purpose flour
6   cups broth
½   cup cream or evaporated milk
Salt and pepper

Brown onion in butter and add flour stirring until smooth. Add broth and milk at same time. Cook to desired thickness. Chop chicken and add to sauce. Serve over your favorite cornbread.

KIM'S CHICKEN CRESCENTS

2   (8 ounce) packages crescent rolls
1   cup Colby cheese
1   can cream of chicken soup
½   cup chopped broccoli
½   cup chopped sweet red pepper
½   cup water chestnuts
¾   cup cooked chicken, chopped
2   tablespoons chopped onion

Unroll each crescent roll and place them in a circle on a baking sheet with the points facing the center. Fill each roll with the above mixture and roll toward the center. Bake at 325 degrees for 25 minutes.

Delicious and great for Christmas.

Kim Miller Thompson
Dalton, Georgia

Entrees

Salads and Dressings

HIGH TECH COTTON

One reason for the increased production of cotton in Georgia has been increased technology, beginning with the Boll Weevil Eradication Program in 1987. It also reflects the growing skills and knowledge that Georgia growers have gained from applied research and techniques and their willingness to invest in new technology.

In addition to equipment advances such as module builders, boll buggies and improved pickers, producers have benefitted from biotechnology. Biotechnology has given farmers genetically engineered cotton which has built-in resistance to insects, greatly reducing the need for pesticides. Cotton that has been engineered to be herbicide-resistant has made it easier for farmers to control weeds without damaging cotton.

Research funded by producers has served to improve growing conditions and educate farmers on topics such as irrigation programs, variety evaluation trials, crop rotations, insect management, weed control, tillage systems and soil fertility. Many of these advances have been made possible with use of Global Positioning Systems (GPS), using satellites to determine crop and soil needs enabling the farmer to manage inputs more precisely.

INDEX

STRAWBERRY NUT SALAD

(A first edition favorite)

2   (3-ounce) packages strawberry gelatin
1   cup chopped nuts
1   (16 -ounce) carton sour cream
2   (10-ounce) packages frozen strawberries, thawed and drained
1   (20-ounce) can crushed pineapple, drained
1   cup boiling water
2   mashed bananas

Dissolve gelatin in boiling water. Add strawberries with juice, drained pineapple, bananas and nuts. Put one half of the mixture into an oblong dish; refrigerate until firm. When congealed, spread sour cream over top. Then pour the other half of the mixture over the sour cream and refrigerate until congealed.

Charlotte Wingate
Doerun, Georgia

CRANBERRY SALAD

2   (3-ounce) package raspberry gelatin
1 ½   cups hot water
1   can whole cranberry sauce
½   cup orange juice
1   cup chopped pecans

Dissolve gelatin in hot water, add cranberry sauce and stir until mixture is smooth. Add pineapple, orange juice and nuts. Stir well and refrigerate overnight.

Myra Kirksey
Byromville, Georgia

DREAM CARROT SALAD

1   (3-ounce) package orange gelatin
1   cup hot water
1   cup grated carrots
1   small can crushed pineapple
1   packaged whipped topping mix (Dream Whip), prepared

Dissolve gelatin in hot water. Drain pineapple, reserving juice. Add enough water to juice to measure ¾ cup. Add liquid to dissolved gelatin. Refrigerate until partially congealed. Add grated carrots and pineapple. Fold in whipped topping. Pour into square casserole dish and refrigerate until firm. Cut into squares to serve. Yield: 8 servings

Nancy Coleman
Hartsfield, Georgia

FROZEN FRUIT SALAD
(A first edition favorite)

1   (8-ounce) package cream cheese
1   cup mayonnaise
1   large can fruit cocktail, drained
1   cup miniature marshmallows
1   small box frozen sliced strawberries, thawed
1   banana, sliced

Cream together cream cheese and mayonnaise. Stir in remaining ingredients. Freeze in loaf pan. Remove from pan; allow to thaw slighting. Slice to serve.

You can also prepare this using muffin pan lined with paper liners. Once frozen, remove the liners and serve on a lettuce leaf.

Lois Clark
Cairo, Georgia

  *Salads and Dressings*

PAPER CUP FROZEN SALAD

2	cups sour cream
1	banana, diced
2	tablespoons lemon juice
4	drops red food coloring
½	cup sugar
¼	cup chopped pecans
⅛	teaspoon salt
1	(16-ounce) can pitted Bing cherries, drained
1	(8-ounce) can crushed pineapple, drained

Combine sour cream, lemon juice, sugar, salt, pineapple, banana, and coloring to give pink tint. Lightly fold in nuts and cherries. Spoon into fluted muffin cups that have been placed in muffin tins. Freeze. Store in plastic bags in freezer. Remove 15 minutes before serving. Peel off paper and place on lettuce leaf. Yield: 12 servings

Leigh Anna Tyus
Moultrie, Georgia

CREAMY FROZEN FRUIT CUPS

1	(8-ounce) package cream cheese, softened
½	cup sugar
1	(10-ounce) jar maraschino cherries, drained
1	(11-ounce) can Mandarin oranges, drained
1	(8-ounce) can crushed pineapple, drained
½	cup chopped pecans
1	(8-ounce) carton frozen whipped topping, thawed

Fresh mint (optional)

In a mixing bowl, beat cream cheese and sugar until fluffy. Halve 9 cherries. Chop the remaining cherries. Set aside the halved cherries and 18 orange sections for garnish. Add the pineapple, pecans, and chopped cherries to the cream cheese mixture. Fold in whipped topping and remaining oranges. Line muffin cups with paper or foil liners. Spoon fruit mixture into cups. Garnish with reserved cherry halves and orange sections. Freeze until firm. Remove 20 minutes before serving. Top with mint, if desired. Yield: 18 servings.

Reba Ledden Milliron
Shellman, Georgia

Salads and Dressings

CROSS CREEK FRUIT SALAD
(A first edition favorite)

Fresh pineapple, cut into bite-sized pieces
Red apples, cored and cut into pieces
Green apples, cored and cut into pieces
Bananas, sliced
Fresh strawberries, sliced
Fresh blueberries or blackberries
Kiwi, peeled and sliced
Nuts, coarsely chopped
Coconut, fresh grated or flaked
Miniature marshmallows

Stir together the above fruits of your choice or add a few. You can make the salad according to your likes and dislikes and according to the number of servings you need.

Dressing:

½	cup sugar
½	cup water
2	tablespoons flour
2	teaspoons butter
1	tablespoon lemon juice

Mix sugar and flour well. Put in small saucepan with butter and water. Bring to a boil over low heat stirring constantly. Remove from heat when thick. Add lemon juice to taste. Cool. Pour over fruit.

Nancy Coleman
Hartsfield, Georgia

FRUIT SALAD

1   can peach pie filling
1   can pineapple chunks, drained
1   pint strawberries, sliced
2   bananas

Combine peach pie filling, drained pineapple chunks, and sliced strawberries. Cover and refrigerate overnight. Just before serving, slice bananas and add to mixture.

Great for coffees during winter months.

Virginia Hart
Moultrie, Georgia

ORANGE-APPLE WALDORF SALAD

1   (2- ounce) can crushed pineapple, undrained
2   tablespoons sugar
1   (3-ounce) package orange gelatin
1   (8 -ounce) package cream cheese, softened and cut up
1   medium apple, cored and chopped
½   cup chopped walnuts
½   (8-ounce) carton frozen whipped topping, thawed

In a medium saucepan, combine undrained pineapple and sugar; heat to boiling. Stir in gelatin until dissolved. Stir in cream cheese until melted and well combined. Remove from heat. Transfer to a large mixing bowl. Chill about 1 hour or until mixture is slightly thickened. Stir in chopped apple and nuts. Fold in whipped topping. Transfer mixture to a 2-quart baking dish or 1 ½ -quart bowl or mold. Cover and chill at least four hours. To serve, cut into squares, serve in bowl or unmold onto serving plate. Yield: 9-12 servings

You can use low-fat cream cheese and whipped topping and sugar-free gelatin. I have used this many times. Our family loves it!

Jane Gibbs
Moultrie, Georgia

MANDARIN ORANGE SALAD

1   (3-ounce) box vanilla instant pudding
1   small can Mandarin oranges, drained
1   large pineapple chunks, reserve juice
4   teaspoons Tang orange-flavored drink mix
2   bananas

Mix juice from pineapple with pudding until dissolved and add Tang. Add Mandarin oranges, bananas and pineapple chunks. Refrigerate until ready to serve.

Mary Walker
Tifton, Georgia

FRESH STRAWBERRY MOUSSE

1   pint fresh strawberries, mashed
2   teaspoons unflavored gelatin
¼   cup confectioner's sugar
2   teaspoons lemon juice
1   pinch salt
1   cup heavy cream

Soften gelatin in 2 tablespoons water. Dissolve gelatin over simmering water. Mix gelatin, mashed strawberries, confectioners' sugar, lemon juice and salt together. Whip cream until it holds shape and fold into strawberry mixture. Freeze mousse in a tray until firm. Serve on lettuce leaf. Yield: 8 servings

Charlotte Mathis
Moultrie, Georgia

  *Salads and Dressings*

CHERRY FLUFF SALAD

1	can cherry pie filling
1	can sweetened condensed milk
1	large can crushed pineapple, drained
1	(16-ounce) carton frozen whipped topping, thawed
½	cup chopped pecans

Mix and pour in bowl and chill.

Myra Kirksey
Byromville, Georgia

GRAPE SALAD

4	pound seedless grapes washed and dried
	(use all red, all green or half red and half green)
8	ounces cream cheese, softened
8	ounces sour cream
1	cup sugar
¾	cup brown sugar
1	teaspoon vanilla

Mix softened cream cheese, sour cream, sugar, brown sugar and vanilla together. Then whip for 5 minutes. Place grapes in bowl and gently mix with cream cheese mixture. Place grape mixture in 9x13-inch glass dish.

Topping:

| 1 | cup brown sugar |
| 1 | cup chopped pecans |

Mix together in a separate bowl. Sprinkle the brown sugar/pecan mixture over the grapes. Refrigerate until ready to serve.

Variations:
+ Substitute a couple of chopped Granny Smith apples for some of the green grapes.
+ Add a cup or so of miniature marshmallows.

Nancy Coleman
Hartsfield, Georgia

GRAPE SALAD

4	cups red grapes
4	cups green grapes
1	cup sour cream
1	(8-ounce) package cream cheese
½	cup sugar
½	cup light brown sugar
1	cup toasted chopped pecans

In a small bowl, mix sour cream, cream cheese and sugar. Pour over grapes and mix well. Place half grape mixture in serving dish and sprinkle with ¼ cup brown sugar and ½ cup toasted nuts. Add the rest of the grape mixture and top with ¼ cup brown sugar and ½ cup nuts. Refrigerate one hour before serving. Yield: 8-10 servings.

Jane Gibbs
Moultrie, Georgia

RAINBOW PASTA SALAD

16	ounces tricolor spiral pasta
2	cups broccoli florets
1	cup chopped carrots
½	cup chopped tomato
½	cup chopped cucumber
½	cup chopped onion
1	(8-ounce) bottle Italian salad dressing

Cook pasta, drain and rinse in cold water. In a large bowl, mix all ingredients and toss to mix. Cover and refrigerate at least 2 hours.

Myra Kirksey
Byromville, Georgia

Salads and Dressings

ORZO SALAD

4 cups chicken broth
1 ½ cups orzo
1 (15-ounce) can garbanzo beans, drained and rinsed
1 ½ cups red and yellow teardrop tomatoes or grape tomatoes, halved
¾ cup finely chopped red onion
½ cup chopped fresh basil leaves
¼ cup chopped fresh mint leaves
About ¾ cup Red Wine Vinaigrette
Salt and freshly ground black pepper

Pour the broth into a large heavy saucepan. Cover the pan and bring the broth to a boil over high heat. Stir in the orzo. Cover partially and cook until the orzo is tender but still firm to the bite, stirring frequently, about 7 minutes. Drain the orzo through a strainer. Transfer the orzo to a large wide bowl and toss until the orzo cools slightly. Set aside to cool completely. Toss the orzo with the beans, tomatoes, onion, basil, mint, and enough vinaigrette to coat. Season the salad, to taste, with salt and pepper, and serve at room temperature.

Red Wine Vinaigrette
½ cup red wine vinegar
¼ cup fresh lemon juice
2 teaspoons honey
2 teaspoons salt
¾ teaspoon freshly ground black pepper
1 cup extra-virgin olive oil

Mix the vinegar, lemon juice, honey, salt, and pepper in a blender. With the machine running, gradually blend in the oil. Season the vinaigrette, to taste, with more salt and pepper, if desired.

This is a wonderful picnic side dish. Orzo is a small pasta that is shaped similar to a large rice grain. It can be found near the spaghetti and other noodle products.

Karen Nikitopoulos, Georgia Cotton Commission
Perry, Georgia

Salads and Dressings

BROCCOLI SALAD

(A first edition favorite)

1	large head broccoli, cut into bite-sized pieces
½	cup raisins or dried cranberries
10	slices bacon, fried and crumbled
5	green onions, minced
1	cup mayonnaise
¼	cup sugar
2	tablespoons red wine vinegar

Mix broccoli, bacon, onions, and raisins. Measure mayonnaise, sugar, and vinegar into a jar. Cover and shake until well mixed. Pour over broccoli mixture and let sit about 8 to 10 hours or overnight. Yield: 8 servings

Nancy Coleman
Hartsfield, Georgia

Linters – the short fuzz on the seed – also are incorporated into high quality paper products such as stationary and currency. According to the Bureau of Engraving and Printing, U.S. paper currency is made up of 75% cotton and 25% linen.

STRAWBERRY SPINACH SALAD
(A first edition favorite)

½   cup pecans
1   (10-ounce) package fresh spinach
1½   cup sliced fresh strawberries

Spread pecans in a shallow pan. Bake at 350 degrees 5 to 7 minutes until toasted. Cool and break in large pieces. Divide torn spinach among 6 salad plates, add layer of strawberries, then sprinkle with chopped nuts. Serve with Poppy Seed Dressing.

Poppy Seed Dressing
¾   cup granulated sugar
1   tablespoon poppy seeds
1   teaspoon dry mustard
½   teaspoon salt
1   teaspoon grated onion
1   cup vegetable oil
⅓   cup cider vinegar

Combine all ingredients in a jar. Cover tightly and shake vigorously. Chill. Can be stored in the refrigerator.

I found this recipe in <u>Progressive Farmer</u> and it is a favorite at our house even with Trey, who is usually not a salad fan.

Virginia Hart
Moultrie, Georgia

STRAWBERRY ROMAINE SALAD

2   heads Romaine lettuce
      (OR 1 Romaine and 1 of another type)
1   pint strawberries, sliced thinly
1   cup (about 4 ounces) Monterey Jack cheese, grated
½   cup toasted, chopped walnuts or pecans

Tear lettuce in small pieces. Add remaining ingredients.

Dressing:
¾   cup sugar
½   cup red wine vinegar
2   cloves garlic, minced
½   teaspoon salt
½   teaspoon paprika
1   cup oil

Dissolve sugar in vinegar before adding oil; blend all ingredients well. May use blender or food processor. This amount of dressing will be enough for 3 or 4 recipes of salad. Pour over lettuce mixture. Yield: 10 servings

Gail Thompson
Moultrie, Georgia

MANDARIN SALAD

¼   cup sliced almonds
1   tablespoon plus 1 teaspoon sugar
¼   head leaf lettuce, torn into bite-size pieces
¼   bunch romaine, torn into bite-size pieces
2   medium stalks celery, chopped (about 1 cup)
2   green onions (with tops), thinly sliced (about 2 tablespoons)
Sweet-Sour Dressing (below)
1   can (11 ounces) Mandarin orange segments, drained real well

Cook almonds and sugar over low heat, stirring constantly, until sugar is melted
and almonds are coated. Cool and break apart. Store at room temperature.
Put celery, onions, and lettuce in large salad bowl. Pour small amount of dressing
and toss. Sprinkle almonds and oranges on top. Yield: 4-6 servings

Sweet-sour Dressing:
     ¼   cup vegetable oil
     2   tablespoons sugar
     2   tablespoons vinegar
     1   tablespoon snipped parsley
     ½   teaspoon salt
     Dash of pepper
     Dash of red pepper sauce

Shake all ingredients in tightly covered jar; refrigerate

Do-ahead Tip: Before dressing is added, salad greens can be closed tightly and
refrigerated no longer than 24 hours.

Pineapple Salad: Substitute 1 can (13 ¼ ounces) pineapple chunk, drained, for
the Mandarin orange segments and snipped mint leaves for the parsley.

Gail Thompson
Moultrie, Georgia

ROMAINE SALAD

3-4   heads of Romaine lettuce, torn into bite-sized pieces

Crunchy Topping:
- 2   packages Ramen noodles, crushed (don't use seasoning packet)
- ½   cup toasted sunflower kernels
- ½   cup sliced almonds
- ½   cup margarine

Melt butter on a baking sheet and stir in other toppings. Bake at 350 degrees until brown. Occasionally stir (about every five minutes) to brown mixture evenly.

Remove from oven and spread out on paper towels to cool.

Sweet and Sour Dressing for Salad:
- 1   cup oil
- 1   cup sugar
- ½   cup apple cider vinegar
- 2   tablespoons soy sauce

Combine all ingredients and stir with wire whisk or shake well. It takes a while to get the sugar to mix up. If you don't serve the dressing right away, plan to shake or stir it again before serving. Just before serving, toss together lettuce, dressings and crunchy topping. Or serve all separately to be added as desired. Yield: 20 servings

Vary the salad by slicing strawberries into it. I've also had it with Mandarin oranges added. Both are yummy. Be careful because the topping can quickly burn. I just crush the Ramen noodles in a gallon zip-top bag, dump in the seeds/nuts, shake, and then place on a pan with margarine or butter.

Julie Rucker
Tifton, Georgia

Salads and Dressings

BLUE CHEESE SLAW

1	head green cabbage
1	cup chopped green onion (more or less, as you like)
1	handful finely chopped fresh Italian parsley leaves (optional)
½	cup mayonnaise
¼	cup red wine vinegar

Salt and freshly ground black pepper to taste

| ¼ | block crumbled blue cheese |

For presentation, line a serving bowl with washed and dried outer cabbage leaves (if in good condition) and set aside. Shred cabbage, preferably in processor and place in a large mixing bowl. Reserve some chopped onion to sprinkle on top for garnish; add remaining chopped onion to the cabbage; mix and set aside. In a small bowl, whisk together the mayonnaise, vinegar, salt, and pepper. Reserve a small amount of the crumbled blue cheese to sprinkle on top for garnish. Add remaining crumbled blue cheese (and parsley) to dressing mix. Season to taste. Pour over the cabbage and toss together well. Cover the bowl with plastic wrap and refrigerate for 2 to 3 hours to allow the flavors to marry. Season to taste. Place in slaw in serving bowl, garnish with blue cheese crumbles and green onions. Serve cold or at room temperature. Yield: 6 to 8 servings.

Karen Nikitopoulos
Georgia Cotton Commission
Perry, Georgia

ZUCCHINI SALAD

3   small zucchini, cut into very thin slices
2   tomatoes, cut into thin wedges
½   green pepper, seeded and cut into thin strips
2   scallions, thinly sliced
French salad dressing

Toss all above together with French dressing and chill for 1 hour. Yield: 6 servings

A tasty, healthy use for our local zucchini.

Charlotte Mathis
Moultrie, Georgia

When cotton is picked in the field in the fall, it is stored in modules which look like giant loaves of bread. Each module holds 13 to 15 500-pound bales, approximately 7500 pounds or about 3 tons. Modules allow the cotton to be stored in the field or at the gin before ginning without loosing yield or quality.

ORIENTAL SALAD

1   (17-ounce) can tiny peas
1   large onion, thinly sliced
1   (16-ounce) can bean sprouts
1   cup chopped celery
1   (12-ounce) can whole kernel white corn
2   (5-ounce) cans water chestnuts
1   (6-ounce) can sliced mushrooms
1   (4-ounce) jar pimentos, sliced
1   large green pepper, thinly sliced
1   cup salad oil
1   cup water
1   cup sugar
½   cup vinegar

Drain the cans and jar of vegetables. Combine with green pepper, onion and celery in a large bowl. Mix oil, water, sugar, and vinegar together. Pour over vegetables, stirring gently. Cover and chill 24 hours; drain before serving. Makes a large amount. Yield: 18-20 servings

Cindy Tyus
Moultrie, Georgia

FANTASTIC POTATO SALAD

12	medium white potatoes (about 5 pounds)
2	tablespoons cider vinegar
2	tablespoons margarine, melted
2	tablespoons sugar
2	teaspoons salt
1	bunch celery, chopped
12	hard-boiled eggs, sliced
1	cup minced parsley
2	(4ounce) jars chopped pimientos
½	cup minced onion
1	(10-ounce) jar sweet pickle relish

Boil potatoes in skins until tender. While hot, peel, cube and toss potatoes lightly with vinegar, margarine, sugar, and salt mixture. Refrigerate until thoroughly chilled, preferably overnight. Add eggs, celery, parsley, pimientos, onion and pickle relish. (Be sure to drain the pickles and pimiento in a sieve because there was too much liquid in the salad otherwise). Chill until flavors blend. Moisten with chilled Mayonnaise-Horseradish Sauce 1 hour before serving. Yield: 20 -25 servings

Mayonnaise-Horseradish Sauce:
1	quart mayonnaise
1	(5-ounce) jar prepared horseradish

Mix well and refrigerate. This sauce is also very good on roast beef or corned beef.

Nancy Coleman
Hartsfield, Georgia

VEGETABLE SALAD

¾ cup white vinegar
1 cup sugar
1 teaspoon salt
½ cup vegetable oil
1 teaspoon pepper
1 (11-ounce) cans white shoe peg corn, drained
1 (15-ounce) can sweet English peas, drained
1 (14.5-ounce) can French-style green beans, drained
1 cup diced green bell pepper
1 cup diced celery
1 cup chopped onion
1 (2-ounce) jar diced pimiento, drained

Bring vinegar, sugar, salt, oil and pepper to boil in a small saucepan over medium-high heat, stirring until sugar dissolves. Cool. Combine vegetables in a large bowl; stir in vinegar mixture. Chill 8 hours; drain. Yield: 10-12 servings.

Virginia Hart
Moultrie, Georgia

LAYERED SALAD

1 head lettuce, chopped
1 medium onion, sliced
1 package frozen small English peas
1 can sliced water chestnuts
1 bell pepper, chopped
2 stalks celery, chopped
2 cups mayonnaise
Bacon bits
Shredded cheese

Layer ingredients in order listed in 9x13-inch casserole dish. Top with mayonnaise, shredded cheese, and bacon bits. Cover and refrigerated overnight.

My sister, Vivian Morrison, gave me this recipe.

Louise Milliron
Shellman, GA

Salads and Dressings

THOUSAND ISLAND DRESSING

(A first edition favorite)

1	egg
¾	salt
½	paprika
1	cup salad oil
2	tablespoons vinegar

Chopped sweet pickles
Garlic salt
Onion salt
Hard-cooked eggs, chopped
Sugar
Pepper

Blend egg in blender. Add all seasonings and ¼ cup oil. While the blender is running, very slowly add remaining oil in a steady steam. Should be fairly thick. Add chopped pickles, hard cooked eggs, garlic salt, onion salt, pepper and sugar to taste. Add other ingredients to taste. Yield: approximately 1 ½ cups

Nancy Coleman
Hartsfield, Georgia

DILL AND TARRAGON SALAD DRESSING

½	cup olive oil
¼	cup tarragon vinegar
1	tablespoon beau monde
1	tablespoon Accent
1	tablespoon dill weed
1	teaspoon crushed black pepper
¼	teaspoon salt

Place all ingredients in a jar. Cover and shake well. Use as a salad dressing for tossed greens, vegetables and pasta. Can also be used as a marinade for chicken and fish.

From Linda West of Vienna and Sandra Bowen of Cordele who served it at the Georgia Cotton Women officers' Christmas party in 1996.

Nancy Coleman
Hartsfield, Georgia

Salads and Dressings

Soups and Stews

THE FIBER

The lint, as farmers and ginners refer to it, or the fiber, as manu-facturers and consumers call it, is the most widely used fiber in the world. In Georgia in 2007, the fiber yielded 801 pounds per acre, about 1.62 bales. The average weight of a bale of cotton is 480-500 pounds.

One 480-pound bale of cotton produces 215 pairs of jeans or 240 sheets or 690 towels or 1,217 t-shirts or 4,321 socks or 313,600 dollar bills. With a current market share of 52 percent, cotton enjoys a majority share of the fiber market.

Because cotton is a natural fiber, it is soft and highly absorbent, making it useful for everything from cosmetic puffs to baby diapers to bath and kitchen linens. Because cotton "breathes," it is very comfortable to wear. It keeps you cool in the summer and warm in the winter. Its durable quality makes it popular for work clothes and play clothes as in the ever-popular denim.

Cotton does not generate static electricity the way man-made fibers do making it the fabric of choice in situations where that is a problem, such as operating rooms and laboratories.

One of the disadvantages of cotton has been its tendency to wrinkle. No more! With the development of a wrinkle-free resin finish, wrinkle-resistant fabrics have further increased cotton's popularity, particularly in men's shirts and slacks.

INDEX

POTATOES AND BACON SOUP

6-8   potatoes
1   large onion, chopped
1   green pepper, chopped (optional)
1   (12-ounce) package bacon, cut into small pieces
4   tablespoons butter
4   tablespoons flour
Milk
Salt and pepper

Peel potatoes and cut into bite-sized pieces. Cook potatoes, onions, bell pepper, bacon, salt and pepper in water until tender; drain off excess water. In separate saucepan, melt butter; stir in flour making a paste. Gradually add milk stirring well to remove all lumps. Continue adding milk until desired thickness. It will thicken as it cooks so start with a cup or so and add to it. Stir in cooked potatoes and bacon. You may need to add more milk at this point. Serve hot.

Nancy Coleman
Hartsfield, Georgia

O'BRIEN POTATO SOUP

1   (28-ounce) package frozen O'Brien hash brown potatoes
1   (28-ounce) can fat-free chicken broth
1 ¼ ounce package Tony Chachere's White Gravy Mix

Bring potatoes to a boil in the chicken broth. Add gravy mix and cook until potatoes are tender. Yield: 9 servings.

This is a wonderful Weight Watchers soup – only 1 point per cup.

Charlotte Wingate
Doerun, Georgia

POTATO SOUP

1   medium onion, chopped
1   stick margarine
6-8   medium potatoes, diced
1   can cream of chicken soup
2   soup cans of water
Salt and pepper to taste
Garlic salt
1   (8-ounce) package Velveeta cheese
Parsley flakes

Sauté onions in butter. Cover potatoes with water and boil until tender; drain. Add soup and water to potatoes; season to taste. Add cheese just before serving. Top with parsley flakes.

Great for after-church gatherings on a cold Sunday night!

Charlotte Mathis
Moultrie, Georgia

CORN CHOWDER

1   pound sausage, browned and drained (your choice mild, medium or hot)
1   can evaporated milk
1   can water
1   (16-ounce) package frozen whole kernel corn
1   can cream style corn
4   large potatoes, peeled and diced
½   teaspoon basil
Salt and pepper to taste

Boil potatoes until almost done; drain. Combine all ingredients and bring to a boil slowly, stirring often. The milk will scorch quickly if you are not careful. Cook over low heat for 1 hour stirring occasionally.

Margaret Anderson
Meigs, Georgia

CREAM OF BROCCOLI SOUP

1	pound broccoli, fresh or frozen
½	pound butter
1	cup flour
1	quart chicken stock*
1	quart half-and-half
1	teaspoon salt
¼	teaspoon white pepper

Clean broccoli; remove stems. Cut into ½-inch pieces. Steam in ½ cup water until tender. **Do not drain.** Set aside. Melt butter in saucepan over medium heat. Add flour to make a roux. Cook for 2-4 minutes. Add chicken stock, stirring with a wire whip, and bring to a boil. Turn heat to low. Add broccoli, half-and-half, salt and pepper. Heat but do not boil. Yield: 8-10 servings

*Homemade or canned stock or 4 bouillon cubes dissolved in a quart of hot water.

We grew broccoli __one__ year. This wonderful soup is my only good memory!

Virginia Hart
Moultrie, Georgia

TURNIP SOUP

4	cups boiling water
3	chicken bouillon cubes or chicken broth
4	medium Irish potatoes, peeled and cubed
1	can turnips
1	can bean and bacon soup
1	cup thick deli sliced ham, cubed

Combine all ingredients except ham in large Dutch oven pot. Cook until potatoes are done. Add cubed ham a few minutes before serving, just long enough to get it to a good warm temperature for eating. (Ham will be tough if cooked too long).

Louise Milliron,
Shellman, Georgia

FRESH VEGETABLE SOUP

(A first edition favorite)

4	quarts water
4	cups smoked ham or smoked picnic shoulder, chopped in bite-size pieces
5	cups fresh butterbeans or 1 (32 ounce) bag frozen butterbeans
2	cups fresh or frozen whole kernel corn
2	cups cream-style fresh or frozen corn
4	(16-ounce) cans whole tomatoes OR
2	quarts fresh stewed tomatoes
4	cups cut-up fresh okra or 2 (1-pound) bags frozen okra
1	tablespoon salt or to taste

Pepper to taste

In large pot, combine water, chopped ham and butterbeans. Cook until beans are tender. Add corn and tomatoes and cook about 30 minutes (stir several times to keep corn from sticking). Add okra and salt. Cook until all ingredients are tender. Yield: approximately 8 quarts. Can be frozen and served later.

From Thomas' mother, Ilene Coleman. I know she loves me when she sends home this soup. I prefer to use 1 (14 ounce) can diced tomatoes, 1 (28 ounce) can diced tomatoes and 1 (28 ounce) can crushed tomatoes.

Nancy Coleman
Hartsfield, Georgia

CAMPFIRE STEW

1 to 2 pounds ground beef
1	large onion, chopped
3	cans Campbell's Vegetarian Vegetable soup

In an iron pot, brown beef and onions. Drain fat. Add soup. Simmer over campfire. If you don't have a campfire handy, a range top will do.

This is an old Girl Scout recipe. A quick and easy supper, especially in winter.

Lois Clark
Cairo, Georgia

SANTE FE SOUP

2	medium onions, chopped
4	pounds raw lean ground beef
1	(5-ounce) package ranch-style dressing mix
1	(5-ounce) package taco seasoning mix
32	ounces canned black beans
32	ounces canned kidney beans
32	ounces canned pinto beans
32	ounces canned tomatoes with green chilies
32	ounces canned diced tomatoes
32	ounces canned white corn
4	cups water

Cook meat and onion together until meat is browned. Stir in ranch-style dressing mix and taco seasoning mix into meat. Add remaining ingredients (beans and tomatoes) with juices from all. Add water. Simmer 2 hours (If mixture is too thick, add additional water. Yield: 32 servings.

This is a wonderful Weight Watcher soup. One serving (1 cup) is 4 points.

Charlotte Wingate
Doerun, Georgia

U. S. textile mills have spun almost 5 million bales of cotton on average for the past three years (2006-2008), enough to make over 1 billion pairs of jeans.

IRISH STEW

(A first edition favorite)

2   pounds all-meat stew beef, cut in bite size pieces
5   cups potatoes cut in small cubes (about 7-8 potatoes)
1   (16-ounce) can diced carrots or frozen carrots
2   large onions, chopped
3   (16-ounce) cans whole tomatoes, mashed
4   cups water
Salt and pepper to taste

Cook stew beef in water until tender. Add remaining ingredients and cook until potatoes are tender. Some of the potatoes should cook to pieces to thicken the stew.

Ilene Coleman
Moultrie, Georgia

FRENCH MARKET SOUP

1   package dried 15-bean soup mix
2   quarts water
1   (16-ounce) package smoked sausage, cut into bite-sized pieces
1   can tomatoes, chopped
1   large onion, chopped
1   tablespoon garlic salt
1¼   teaspoon salt
½   teaspoon pepper

Sort and wash beans; soak overnight. Drain beans; add water, sausage, salt, tomatoes, onion, garlic salt, and pepper. Cover; bring to boil. Reduce heat and simmer for 2½ hours. Stir occasionally. Serve with hot cornbread.

Steve Tyus
Moultrie, Georgia

CHICKEN TORTILLA SOUP

1   onion, chopped
3   cloves garlic, minced
1   tablespoon olive oil
2   teaspoons chili powder
1   teaspoon cumin
1   teaspoon garlic powder
1   (28-ounce) can crushed tomatoes
5   (10.5-ounce) cans condensed chicken broth
2 ¼   cups water
1   cup whole corn kernels, cooked
1   cup white hominy
1   (4-ounce) can chopped green chili peppers
1   (15-ounce) can black beans, rinsed and drained
¼   cup chopped fresh cilantro
2   boneless chicken breast halves, cooked and shredded

Garnish soup according to your taste:
    Crushed tortilla chips
    Sliced avocado (or guacamole)
    Shredded Monterey Jack cheese
    Chopped green onions
    Sour cream

In a medium stock pot, heat oil over medium heat. Sauté onion and garlic in oil until soft. Stir in chili powder, cumin, garlic powder, tomatoes, broth, and water. Bring to a boil, and simmer for at least 1 hour. Stir in corn, hominy, chilies, beans, cilantro, and chicken. Simmer for 15 minutes. Ladle soup into individual serving bowls, and top with crushed tortilla chips, avocado slices (or guacamole), cheese, sour cream and chopped green onion.

Lindsey Walker Kaiser
Tifton, Georgia

CHICKEN TACO SOUP

(A first edition favorite)

2   boneless, skinless chicken breasts
1   teaspoon olive oil
1   large onion, chopped
¼   teaspoon minced garlic (or more)
½   teaspoon chili powder
¼   teaspoon ground cumin
2   tablespoons lime juice
1   cup salsa
2   (14½ -ounce) cans fat-free chicken broth
Tortilla or taco chips, optional
Grated Cheddar or Monterey Jack cheese

Cut chicken into bite-size pieces. Heat olive oil in Dutch oven or large sauce pot. Add chicken and cook on high until brown, about 2 minutes. Add onion, garlic, cumin and chili powder; cook ten minutes, until onion is tender. Add lime juice, salsa and chicken broth. Heat to boiling and then reduce to simmer. Simmer, covered 8 to 10 minutes. Sprinkle with grated cheese and crumbled tortilla chips. Yield: 4 servings.

This is sooo good. It's my family's favorite soup. Quick and easy to prepare. We like more "soup," so I add extra broth.

Nancy Coleman
Hartsfield, Georgia

Soups and Stews

SLOWED COOKED CHILI

(A first edition favorite)

2   (16-ounce) can red kidney beans, drained
2   (14 ½ -ounce) cans tomatoes, cut up
2   pounds coarsely ground beef or beef stew cut into small pieces
2   medium onions, coarsely chopped
1   green pepper, coarsely chopped
2   cloves garlic, crushed OR equivalent garlic powder
2 to 3 tablespoons chili powder
1   teaspoon pepper
1   teaspoon cumin
Salt to taste
Cheddar cheese, grated

Brown beef and drain off fat. Spray crock pot with cooking spray. Put all ingredients in crock-pot in order listed. Stir once. Cover and cook on low 10 to 12 hours or on high 5 to 6 hours or until meat and vegetables are to desired tenderness. Serve with grated cheese and additional chopped onions, if desired. If you don't have a crock pot, you can cook on top of stove if you use ground beef. Yield: 8 to 10 servings.

Excellent. Smells wonderful while cooking. Best chili I've ever eaten and so easy.

Nancy Coleman
Hartsfield, Georgia

WHITE CHICKEN CHILI

3   tablespoons olive oil
1   medium onion, finely chopped
1   (14-ounce) can chopped green chilies, drained
3   tablespoons all-purpose flour
2   teaspoons ground cumin
2   (16-ounce) cans Navy or Great Northern beans
1   (14.5-ounce) can chicken broth
1½ cups finely chopped cooked chicken breasts
Shredded Monterey Jack cheese, optional
Sour cream, optional
Salsa, optional

In large skillet, cook onion in oil for 4 minutes or until tender and transparent. Add chilies, flour and cumin; cook and stir for 2 minutes. Add beans and chicken broth; bring to boil. Reduce heat; simmer for 10 minutes or until thickened. Add chicken; cook until chicken is hot. Garnish with cheese, sour cream and salsa, if desired.

My family loves soups. This is one of our newest favorites.

Nancy Coleman
Hartsfield, Georgia

Soups and Stews

SHRIMP STEW

(A favorite from the first edition)

Vegetable oil
3   stalks celery
All-purpose flour
5   pounds shrimp, peeled
1   large onion
2   large bell peppers
2   (8-ounce) cans tomato sauce

Sauté onions, celery and bell peppers in a small amount of oil on medium heat. Stir in about 2 tablespoons of flour and blend until smooth. Add tomato sauce and remove from heat. In a large sauce pan, add shrimp to boiling water; return to boiling. Add tomato mixture to shrimp and cook on low approximately 3 hours. The longer it cooks, the better!

Charlotte Wingate
Doerun, Georgia

OYSTER OR SALMON STEW

¼   cup (½ stick) butter
1   onion, chopped
Milk
1   pint oysters OR 1 can salmon

Melt butter in large saucepan or Dutch oven. Sauté onions until tender. If using oysters, wash oysters thoroughly to remove shells and other foreign matter. Pour oysters or salmon in with onion and sauté until edges of oysters curl. Add 3 to 4 cups milk. Simmer but do not allow to boil. Serve hot with saltine crackers.

My mother always made oyster stew, but Thomas' mother always made salmon stew. I had never eaten salmon stew until we got married, but we like it just as well as oyster stew. And we almost always have a can of salmon in the cabinet for a quick and easy supper on a cool night.

Nancy Coleman
Hartsfield, Georgia

Vegetables and Side Dishes

THE SEED

Cotton is nature's food and fiber plant. After harvest, the lint is separated from the seeds. The lint is baled for used in textiles while the seed is used for a variety of purposes. For each 100 pounds of fiber, the plants produce 132 pounds of seed. If an acre of cotton produces about 800 pounds of fiber, it would yield 1,050 pounds of seed.

Cottonseed oil, America's first vegetable oil, is extracted from cottonseed at large crushing mills. The extracted oil is then purified through a refining process. Cottonseed oil, which contains no cholesterol, is used in shortening, margarine, cooking oil and salad dressing. Cottonseed oil is also one of the most widely used oils in the lucrative snack food market.

Cottonseed meal and hulls are used as livestock, poultry and fish feed. It is also used as a fertilizer.

Cellulose from the linters (tiny short fibers that stick to the hull of the cottonseed) is used for making plastics, rocket propellants, rayon, pharmaceutical emulsions, cosmetics, photography and x-ray film, and upholstery. Linters also are incorporated into high quality paper products such as stationary and currency. According to the Bureau of Engraving and Printing, U.S. paper currency is made up of 75% cotton and 25% linen.

INDEX

Vegetables and Side Dishes

CHEESE GRITS
(A first edition favorite)

6   **cups boiling water**
1½   **cup grits (not instant grits)**
2   **teaspoons salt**
½   **cup (1 stick) butter or margarine**
1½   **pounds (24 ounces) grated Cheddar cheese**

Slowly stir grits into boiling water, stirring constantly. Reduce heat and cook in covered saucepan until thickened, about 8 minutes. Add grated cheese and butter.

What's a good Southern fish fry without Cheese Grits?

Ilene Coleman
Moultrie, Georgia

In 2007, Georgia producers planted 1,030,000 acres of cotton with a yield of almost 1.7 million bales of cotton and an estimated value of $745 million dollars.

MACARONI AND CHEESE

1 ½ cups elbow macaroni noodles
Salt and pepper
1   cup mild Cheddar cheese
1   cup sharp Cheddar cheese
1   cup milk
1   egg
1   teaspoon prepared mustard
½   teaspoon Worcestershire sauce
1   small jar Cheese Whiz

Heat oven to 350 degrees. Cook macaroni by box directions. Drain. Spray bottom of 8x8-inch baking dish with cooking spray. Salt and pepper bottom of pan. Pour half the macaroni noodles in dish. Salt and pepper noodles. Sprinkle with ½ cup mild cheese and ½ cup sharp cheese. Layer the rest of the noodles, salt and pepper then, and add the rest of the mild cheese and sharp cheese. Mix together the milk, egg, mustard and Worcestershire sauce and heat in microwave for 30 seconds. Heat Cheese Whiz in microwave for 45 seconds and whisk together with the milk mixture. Pour over top of noodles. Salt and pepper the top. Bake uncovered for 45 minutes to an hour. Yield: 6 ½ cup servings

A friend, Dawn Pridgen, shared this recipe with me. Delicious! I use whole wheat noodles and reduced fat cheese to make it a little healthier.

Sandra Moretz
Chula, Georgia

Full-fat cheese melts better than lower fat varieties. Freshly grated cheese also melts better than packaged grated cheese.

Vegetables and Side Dishes

BAKED MACARONI AND CHEESE

1   (8-ounce) box elbow macaroni
1   pound grated Cheddar cheese
1   stick butter or margarine
2   cups milk
1   egg, beaten
Salt and pepper to taste

Boil macaroni according to package directions under tender; drain leaving just enough water to cover the top of the macaroni. Add butter, 1 cup of milk and about one-fourth of the cheese to the hot pasta. Stir until cheese and butter are melted. Place half the macroni mixture in a casserole dish. Cover with half the remaining cheese, patting the cheese into the noodles. Layer remaining macaroni and grated cheese. Pat cheese into noodles so cheese is covered with milk. Bake at 350 degrees until mixture bubbles, about 30 minutes. Mix egg and remaining 1 cup of milk. Pour over macaroni and cheese. Return to oven and bake until top is brown and mixture is set.

My family loves this dish. I cook it every time we all get together.

Ilene Coleman
Moultrie, Georgia

CHEESY APPLE CASSEROLE

2   (20-ounce) cans sliced apples (not pie filling)
½   cup (1 stick) butter, sliced
1   cup sugar
¾   cup all-purpose flour
1   (8-ounce) package Velveeta cheese, grated

Drain apples and spread in a greased 9x13-inch glass baking dish. Combine butter, sugar, flour and cheese. Drop by spoonful on apples. Bake at 350 degrees fro 30 minutes.

Nancy Coleman
Hartsfield, Georgia

ASPARAGUS CASSEROLE
(A first edition favorite)

1	large can asparagus
1	large can English peas
1	can cream of mushroom soup
6	slices bread
2	cups grated Cheddar cheese

Drain peas and asparagus; save asparagus juice. In baking dish, spread cream of mushroom soup; sprinkle with a layer (one-half can) of peas and then a layer of asparagus (one-half can). Pinch 3 slices of bread in small pieces and dip in asparagus juice and place on top of asparagus. Sprinkle with half the cheese. Repeat layers. Top with balance of cheese. Bake at 350 degrees until mixture bubbles and cheese is lightly browned.

Ilene Coleman
Moultrie, Georgia

BARBECUED BAKED BEANS
(A first edition favorite)

¼	cup butter
1	large onion, chopped
1	bell pepper, chopped (optional)
1	cup ketchup
¼	cup firmly packed brown sugar
3	tablespoons Worcestershire sauce
1	teaspoon salt
⅛	teaspoon pepper
1½	teaspoons chili powder
1	gallon pork and beans, drained
1	pound sliced bacon

Melt butter in saucepan. Add onion and bell pepper and sauté until tender; stir in remaining ingredients except beans and bacon. Cover and simmer at least 5 minutes. Mix beans and sauce in large pot or mixing bowl. Pour beans into two 9x13-inch casserole dishes or one very large dish. Top with bacon. Bake one hour at 325 degrees or until beans are very bubbly and bacon is done. Yield: 20 servings.

Nancy Coleman
Hartsfield, Georgia

Vegetables and Side Dishes

BAKED BEANS

2   (16-ounce) cans Bush's Original Baked Beans, drained
½   cup chopped onion
1   tablespoon light margarine (in the tub)
½   cup ketchup
2   tablespoon prepared mustard
1   tablespoon Worcestershire sauce
½   cup brown sugar
¼   cup real bacon bits

Heat oven to 350 degrees. Sauté onion in margarine until soft. Stir all ingredients together and place in oven proof baking dish. Bake uncovered for 45 minutes to 1 hour.

Sandra Moretz
Chula, Georgia

HARVARD BEETS

3   cans whole beets (sliced beets may be used)
¾   cup sugar
1   tablespoon cornstarch
½   cup water
¼   cup vinegar
2   tablespoons butter

Mix sugar and cornstarch in sauce pan. Add vinegar and water and boil for 5 minutes. Add beets to hot sauce. Just before serving, add butter and return to a boil.

Mary B. Smith
Brinson, Georgia

BROCCOLI WITH CHIPOTLE LIME BUTTER

1 ½   pounds broccoli
¼   cup butter
1   tablespoon fresh lime juice
1   teaspoon ground chipotle pepper

Place a steamer basket in a large saucepan. Add water to just below the bottom of the basket. Bring water to boiling. Add broccoli. Cover and steam for 8-10 minutes until desired doneness. In a serving bowl, stir together melted butter, lime juice and pepper. Add broccoli; toss to coat. Season with salt. Serve immediately. Yield: 6 servings.

The butter mixture can be used on other fresh vegetables, like corn on the cob.

Nancy Coleman
Hartsfield, Georgia

BROCCOLI AND RICE CASSEROLE

2   (8-ounce) packages of frozen chopped broccoli
¾   stick margarine
2   large onions, chopped
¾   cup instant rice, uncooked
1   can cream of mushroom soup
2   cups grated Cheddar cheese

Defrost broccoli in microwave (don't drain). Combine margarine and onions and cook in microwave until onions are translucent. Combine onions, broccoli, cream of mushroom soup, the uncooked rice and one cup of grated cheese. Salt and pepper to taste and top with the last cup of grated cheese. Bake at 350 degrees for about 30-35 minutes.

Patsy Wester
Meigs, Georgia

Vegetables and Side Dishes

BROCCOLI CASSEROLE

(A first edition favorite)

2	packages frozen broccoli
1	can cream of mushroom soup
2	eggs
1	cup mayonnaise
1½	cup grated cheese

Thaw packages of broccoli. Drain off liquid. You want it as dry as possible. Stir together the soup, eggs, and mayonnaise. Spray a square casserole dish with cooking spray. Layer half of broccoli in dish. Cover with half of cream mixture. Repeat with other half of broccoli and the rest of cream mixture. Bake at 325 degrees approximately 40 minutes. Top with the grated cheese the last 5 minutes of baking.

Linda Stripling
Moultrie, Georgia

GLORIFIED CABBAGE

1	medium head cabbage
1	onion, chopped
½	pound Velveeta, cut into cubes
¼	cup margarine
1	can cream of mushroom soup
2	cups bread crumbs

Chop and boil cabbage until tender; drain. Sauté onion in margarine. Add soup and stir until smooth. Add cheese and stir until cheese is melted and mixture is smooth. Mix with drained cabbage. Pour into a prepared casserole dish. Top with bread crumbs. Bake for 20 minutes.

Nancy Coleman
Hartsfield, Georgia

MARINATED CABBAGE

(A favorite from the first edition)

1   head cabbage
1   onion
1   bell pepper
1   cup sugar

Slice cabbage in a large bowl; then slice onion and bell pepper on top of cabbage. Pour the sugar over this mixture; set aside.

Dressing:
1   tablespoon salt
1   teaspoon celery seed
1   teaspoon dry mustard
1   cup white vinegar
¾   cup salad oil

Combine all ingredients in a saucepan and bring this mixture to a boil. Pour over cabbage mixture. DO NOT STIR. Cover and let set overnight in the refrigerator.

Charlotte Wingate
Doerun, Georgia

  *Vegetables and Side Dishes*

PAN FRIED CORN

12   ears Silver Queen corn
Butter
3 - 4 strips streak o' lean (or bacon)

Wash corn; grate the kernels off. Put a little butter in a cast iron skillet and fry up
3-4 strips of streak o' lean (or bacon). When the streak o' lean is nice and brown,
take it out; add a stick of butter to the drippings. Then pour in the corn kernels;
stir and fry them until done, about 5 to 8 minutes. Chop up the meat and throw
it back in the corn. Season with salt and pepper. Yield: 6 to 8 servings

Charlotte Wingate
Doerun, Georgia

EGGPLANT EN CASSEROLE
(A first edition favorite)

1   medium eggplant
1   onion, sliced
3   tomatoes, sliced
1   cup grated cheese
6   tablespoons margarine, melted
2   green peppers, sliced
Salt and pepper to taste

Peel and slice eggplant; fry in margarine. Place in casserole with alternate layers of
sliced onion, green peppers and tomatoes. Sprinkle each layer with salt and pepper. Cover and bake at 350 degrees for 1 hour until eggplant is tender. Uncover
and sprinkle with cheese. Return to oven to melt cheese, 5 to 10 minutes.

Charlotte Mathis
Moultrie, Georgia

Vegetables and Side Dishes

BASIL GREEN BEANS

1	(128 oz.) can green beans (or equivalent in smaller cans)
¼	cup sugar
1	cup butter, melted
2	teaspoons salt
1	teaspoon pepper
6	teaspoons fresh basil
1	tablespoon garlic powder

Simmer green beans for 10 minutes and drain. Combine all other ingredients. Pour over beans. Simmer 10 minutes and steam until tender but not mushy. Yield: 15 servings

Fresh or frozen green beans can be used but should be cooked until almost tender.

Nancy Coleman
Hartsfield, Georgia

CREOLE GREEN BEANS

1	pound fresh string beans, stems ends removed
1	tablespoon vegetable oil
1	teaspoon Old Bay Blackened Seasoning
½	cup pecan pieces

Salt to taste

Bring a large pot of water to boil. Add green beans, return to a boil and cook 1 minute; the beans should still be crisp. Drain the beans; don't rinse. In a large skillet, add oil. Heat until very hot (the skillet is ready when a drop of water in the oil sizzles.) Add beans and cook about 1 minute, turning often with tongs or spatula. Sprinkle on pecans and Old Bay seasoning. Turn beans and pecans to coat with oil and seasoning; cook about 2 minutes more, or until beans and nuts are slightly browned. Salt to taste and serve. Yield: 4 servings.

Nancy Coleman
Hartsfield, Georgia

SOUTHERN GREEN BEAN BUNDLES

2	cans whole green beans
1	pound bacon
¾	stick butter
½	cup brown sugar

Salt
Pepper
Garlic salt

Hold beans in hand (as many as you can hold) all laying in the same direction. Wrap bacon around beans and place in casserole dish. Makes about 8 bundles. Melt butter; add brown sugar and stir until melted. Pour mixture over bundles. Salt, pepper and garlic salt to taste. Cook, covered, at 350 degrees for 45 minutes; uncover and cook 15 minutes or until bacon browns.

Less time consuming: Drain beans. Place in casserole dish. Pour melted butter and sugar over beans. Layer strips of bacon over beans. Bake as directed. After 45 minutes, remove bacon and microwave bacon until crisp. Crumble bacon and sprinkle over beans before serving. Yield: 8 servings.

Virginia Hart
Moultrie, Georgia

GREEN BEAN BUNDLES

1	(16-ounce) can whole green beans or 3 cups fresh green beans, cooked

Bacon slices

1	(8-ounce) bottle Catalina dressing
5	pieces bacon, halved, partially cooked, and drained

Drain beans and divide into bundles of 5-7 beans. Wrap each bundle with ½ piece of bacon. Place in a glass dish. Pour dressing over beans and marinate for several hours. Bake 20 minutes at 350 degrees.

Brenda Morris
Ocilla, Georgia

HOLIDAY GREEN BEANS

2	cans French style green beans
½	stick margarine
1	tablespoon sugar
½	teaspoon salt
1	teaspoon dried basil
¾	teaspoon garlic salt
¼	teaspoon pepper
2	tablespoons chopped onions
2	cups cherry tomatoes, halved

Cook beans and onion in the liquid from the beans for 15-20 minutes. Drain well. Melt butter and add other seasonings. Pour this over green beans and simmer 5 minutes. Stir in tomatoes right before serving. The tomatoes should not be mushy. Yield: 6-8 servings. Can easily be doubled.

This has been used for many Christmas dinners. Very pretty and tasty. A different way to serve green beans, and not just at Christmas.

Jane Gibbs
Moultrie, Georgia

SESAME GREEN BEANS

1	(1 pound) bag frozen whole or Italian cut green beans
8-10	strips of bacon
½	teaspoon crushed red pepper flakes
2	tablespoons toasted sesame seeds (a handful)
Coarse salt	

Cook beans in microwave according to package directions; drain. Cook bacon in skillet until crispy; remove from pan and drain on paper towels; reserve drippings. Add cooked green beans and red pepper flakes to bacon drippings and cook until almost browned. (You may need to add additional bacon drippings or vegetable oil to the pan.). Add sesame seeds and coarse salt and toss to coat beans evenly.

If you don't have sesame seeds, the beans are just as good without them.

Nancy Coleman
Hartsfield, Georgia

Vegetables and Side Dishes

SWEET AND SPICY GREEN BEANS

5   (14.5 ounce) cans Blue Lake green beans
¾   cup butter
¼   teaspoon garlic salt
1   dash Worcestershire sauce
1   cup light brown sugar
Sliced bacon

Melt butter with garlic salt and Worcestershire sauce in large baking dish. Add green beans and mix well. Sprinkle brown sugar over beans. Place bacon slices over beans. Back 30-45 minutes until bacon is done. For ease of serving, cut the bacon strips in thirds before putting on beans. Yield: 15 servings

Suellen Perry
Moultrie, Georgia

SOUTHERN GREEN BEANS

1   (28-ounce) can green beans
1   tablespoon bacon bits
½   teaspoon squeeze margarine
½   teaspoon Garlic & Herb Mrs. Dash
½   teaspoon Better than Bouillon ham base

Drain green beans and add fresh water. Add bacon bits, margarine, Mrs. Dash, and ham base. Bring to a boil. Reduce heat to simmer, cover, and cook 30 minutes or longer. Yield: 7 ½-cup servings

I'm a dietitian and patients often ask how to make green beans taste good without fatback or bacon grease. My family LOVES my green beans!

Sandra Moretz
Chula, Georgia

OKRA OMELET

(A first edition favorite)

2	cups okra, cut crosswise
1	egg
¼	teaspoon black pepper
4	tablespoons bacon drippings
½	cup milk
½	cup hush puppy mix
½	teaspoon Accent
1	teaspoon salt

Mix all ingredients, except bacon drippings, in bowl. Pour bacon drippings into baking pan. Pour all mixture into the pan and pat flat. Bake at 350 degrees for 30 minutes. Turn omelet over and bake 5 to 10 minutes. Cut into serving pieces. Yield: 4 to 6 servings.

I cook mine in a thin, flat iron skillet.

Louise Milliron
Shellman, Georgia

SAUTEED OKRA

Okra, sliced
Oil
Salt and pepper to taste

In a large cast iron skillet, heat oil. Add okra and cook, stirring constantly, until desired doneness. Drain on paper towels. Salt and pepper.

We cook okra more often by this method than any other. Thomas likes his cooked just a little bit so that it's still kind of slimy, but I like mine cooked until crisp and crunchy, almost burned.

Nancy Coleman
Hartsfield, Georgia

Vegetables and Side Dishes

SCALLOPED PINEAPPLE

(A first edition favorite)

4   cups bread cubes (no crust)
1½   cups granulated sugar
3   eggs
1   cup milk
½   cup melted butter
1   (20-ounce) can crushed pineapple with juice

Mix all together and put in a buttered 2-quart casserole. Let stand for a few minutes before baking at 350 degrees for 45 minutes. Yield: 8 generous servings.

This is great with pork and has been a hit at several Young Farmer Annual Banquets in Colquitt County.

Virginia Hart
Moultrie, Georgia

BLENDER POTATO CASSEROLE

1   cup milk
1   cup cubed Cheddar cheese
3   eggs
½   green pepper, diced (optional)
1 ½ teaspoon salt
1   small onion, diced or quartered
½   teaspoon pepper
4   medium potatoes, peeled, cubed and uncooked
2   tablespoons butter

Combine all ingredients in a blender in order listed, cover and blend on high speed just until potatoes go through the blades (do not over blend). Pour the mixture into a greased 1½- quart casserole dish and bake uncovered at 350 degrees for 50 minutes to 1 hour.

Yvonne H. Crawford
Tifton, Georgia

CHEESY-CHIVE POTATOES

4   medium potatoes, cooked and diced
1   cup sour cream
1   cup small curd cottage cheese
1   teaspoon chives
½   teaspoon garlic powder
½   teaspoon salt
½   teaspoon white pepper
1   cup grated sharp Cheddar cheese

Combine all ingredients. Place in lightly greased casserole dish. You may sprinkle with paprika if so desired. Bake at 350 degrees for 30 minutes.

Brenda Morris
Ocilla, Georgia

HASH BROWN CHEESE BAKE

1   (32-ounce) package frozen shredded hash browns, thawed
2   cans potato soup, undiluted
1   8-ounce carton sour cream
2   cups grated sharp Cheddar cheese
1   cup grated Parmesan cheese

Combine all ingredients, spoon into a greased 13x9-inch baking dish and bake at 350 degrees for 40 minutes. Yield: 12-15 servings.

Myra Kirksey
Byromville, Georgia

HASH BROWN POTATO CASSEROLE

1	(2-pound) package frozen cubed hash browns
1½	teaspoons salt
½	teaspoon black pepper
1	can cream of chicken soup
½	cup chopped onions
1	pint sour cream
1	(16-ounce) package grated Cheddar cheese
1	small jar chopped pimentos
¼	cup margarine
2	cups corn flakes

Thaw potatoes. Separate. Mix hash browns, salt, pepper, soup, onions, sour cream, Cheddar cheese, and pimentos together. Spread in 9x13-inch baking dish. Melt margarine and mix with corn flakes. Top casserole with flakes and bake at 350 degrees for 1 hour.

My sister, Vivian Morrison, from Cusseta, Georgia, gave me this recipe.

Louise Milliron
Shellman, Georgia

APPLE CHEESE CASSEROLE

1	can White House sliced apples
8	ounces Velveeta cheese
¾	stick margarine
1	cup sugar
¾	cup flour
¼	cup evaporated milk

Cream margarine, sugar, flour, and cheese. Place apples in a baking dish and press cheese mixture over and into apples. Pour milk or cream over the apples and bake at 350 degrees for 30 minutes. Sprinkle cinnamon on top.

I can only find White House apples at Harvey's.

Cathy Thompson
Vienna, Georgia

LOADED MASHED POTATOES

5	pounds potatoes, peeled and cubed
¾	cup sour cream
½	cup milk
3	tablespoons butter

Salt and pepper to taste

3	cups (12-ounces) shredded Cheddar cheese, divided
½	pound sliced bacon, cooked and crumbled
3	green onions, sliced

Place potatoes in Dutch oven and cover with water; bring to boil. Reduce heat; cover and cook for 15-20 minutes or until tender. Drain and place in mixing bowl. Add the sour cream, milk, butter, salt and pepper. Beat on medium-low speed until light and fluffy. Stir in 2 cups cheese, bacon and onion. Pour mixture into greased 3-quart baking dish. Top with remaining cheese. Bake, uncovered, at 350 degrees for 30 minutes or until heated through and cheese is melted. Yield: 14 servings.

Nancy Coleman
Hartsfield, Georgia

MOM'S PARTY POTATOES

5	pounds potatoes (peeled, cooked and creamed)
½	cup butter
8	ounces cream cheese
1	cup sour cream
½	cup Parmesan cheese
4	spring onions, chopped
1	tablespoon salt

Add all ingredients together in baking dish and top with shredded cheese. Bake at 350 degrees for 20 minutes.

Maurissa Smith
Atlanta, Georgia

Vegetables and Side Dishes

TWICE BAKED POTATOES
(A first edition favorite)

4	medium baking potatoes
2	sticks margarine, softened
½	cup bacon bits
½	cup sour cream
1	small onion, finely chopped
¼	cup milk

Season salt
Pepper
Garlic salt
Shredded cheese
Paprika

Bake potatoes. Slice lengthwise and scoop out middles. Mix potato middles with all ingredients except cheese and paprika. Fill potato shells and top with cheese and paprika. Bake in oven until cheese is melted.

Susan York
Pavo, Georgia

PARTY POTATOES

8-10 medium to large red potatoes
1   (8-ounce) package cream cheese
1   cup sour cream
Garlic salt
Chives, optional
Paprika

Peel, quarter and cook potatoes until soft; drain. Beat cream cheese and sour cream until smooth. Gradually add hot cooked potatoes to creamed mixture, beating until light and fluffy. If too stiff, thin with milk. Season to taste with garlic salt and chives. Spoon into 2-quart casserole. Brush with melted butter. Sprinkle with paprika. Bake at 350 degrees for 30 minutes.

Connie Mobley*
Moultrie, Georgia

Mrs. Mobley was one of the founders of Georgia Cotton Women. Her husband, the late John M. Mobley, Sr., established the Mobley Scholarship administered by GCW. The scholarship is presented annually to the son, daughter, grandson or granddaughter of a Georgia cotton producer. Mrs. Mobley has continued to sponsor the scholarship after his passing. She remains a cherished member of GCW.

PARMESAN BAKED POTATOES

6   tablespoons margarine
4   tablespoons grated Parmesan cheese
8   medium unpeeled potatoes, halved lengthwise

Pour margarine in 13x9-inch dish, sprinkle cheese over it. Place potatoes, cut side down over cheese. Bake uncovered at 400 degrees for 40-45 minutes.

Myra Kirksey
Byromville, Georgia

Vegetables and Side Dishes

POTATOLICIOUS

(A first edition favorite)

6	large (new) red potatoes
2	large onions
4	tablespoons real butter
1	teaspoon salt
1	(8-ounce) package cream cheese
1	cup sour cream
1	stick real butter
1	tablespoon dried parsley
1	tablespoon dried chives
6	slices thick-sliced Velvetta cheese (cut each slice into 3 parts)

Peel and slice potatoes ¼-inch thick; par-boil in salted water until tender. Drain well. Slice onions and separate into rings; sauté in 4 tablespoons butter until tender and clear. (You may do this while potatoes are cooking, that way both are ready at same time.) In microwave soften cream cheese, sour cream, and stick of butter. Stir well; add parsley and chives. In a casserole or baking dish, layer potatoes, onions, cream cheese mixture and Velvetta cheese. Repeat layers of potatoes, onions, cream cheese mixture and Velvetta cheese. Bake in oven at 350 degrees for 30 minutes, or until cheeses are melted. Sprinkle with more dried parsley and chives. Yield: 6 to 8 servings.

I use a terra-cotta baking dish, and I have to extend the baking time to 45 minutes to 1 hour. I made this recipe up for another Dairilious Cook-Off. I didn't win first-place, too many calories, but all the men involved wanted the recipe (some of the women, too).

Mary Register
Waterloo, Georgia

PESTO POTATOES

1   cup mayonnaise
2   tablespoons prepared pesto
4   cups quartered cooked red potatoes
½   cup chopped celery (optional)
½   cup sliced green onions
½   cup diced red bell peppers
1 ½ cups or 6 ounces Monterey Jack cheese
1   tablespoon Parmesan cheese

In a large bowl, mix mayonnaise, pesto, potatoes, celery, green onion, peppers and Monterey Jack cheese. Lightly sprinkle with Parmesan cheese. Serve warm.

Mary Walker
Tifton, Georgia

SCALLOPED POTATOES
(A first edition favorite)

6-8   medium potatoes, peeled and sliced thin
Butter
Flour
Milk
Salt and pepper

Spray a casserole dish with cooking spray. Place a layer of sliced potatoes in bottom of casserole. Salt and pepper. Sprinkle flour over potatoes. Dot with butter. (Be generous with the butter, but don't over do it.) Repeat layers until all potatoes are used or dish is full. Place dish on baking sheet which has been covered with foil to make cleanup easier in the event of boil over. Fill dish with milk, covering last layer of flour completely. Place dish in oven and bake at 350 degrees for one hour or until potatoes test tender with pricked with fork. Yield: 6 servings.

A favorite when I was growing up. You knew somebody loved you when you got Scalloped Potatoes. A most requested dish by my teenage son. I sometimes sprinkle chopped onions over each layer of potatoes.

Nancy Coleman
Hartsfield, Georgia

Vegetables and Side Dishes

NANA'S SQUASH CASSEROLE

4	cups cooked squash
1	cup mayonnaise
1	can cream of mushroom soup
1	medium onion chopped
2	eggs, slightly beaten
24	crushed saltine crackers
1	cup grated cheese

Add pepper to taste

Mix the cooked squash, mayonnaise, cream of mushroom soup, onion, eggs and saltine crackers (reserve enough saltines for topping). Place in 13x9-inch baking dish. Cover with cheese and top with reserved saltine crackers. Bake at 350 degrees for 30 minutes.

Maurissa Smith
Atlanta, Georgia

POSH SQUASH

2	pounds yellow squash, washed, trimmed and sliced
1	cup mayonnaise
1	cup grated Parmesan cheese
1	small onion, chopped
2	eggs, beaten
½	teaspoon salt
¼	teaspoon pepper
½	cup soft bread crumbs
1	tablespoon butter or margarine

Cook squash, covered, in boiling water for 10-15 minutes or until tender. Drain and cool slightly. Combine mayonnaise, cheese, onion, eggs, salt and pepper. Stir until well combined. Add squash, stirring gently. Pour squash mixture into a lightly greased 1½- quart casserole dish. Combine bread crumbs and butter. Spoon over squash mixture. Bake at 350 degrees for 30 minutes.

Jane Gibbs
Moultrie, Georgia

 *Vegetables and Side Dishes*

SQUASH CASSEROLE

2   cups squash
1   onion, chopped
½   cup milk
1   egg, beaten
Salt and pepper to taste
Saltine or Ritz crackers
Grated cheese, lots

Cook squash with onions until tender; drain off excess water. Add egg, milk, salt and pepper to taste. Crumble a few crackers into mixture. Bake in greased dish at moderate temperature until set. Sprinkle grated cheese on top. Return to oven for cheese to melt.

We eat a lot of squash from the garden and have tried several recipes over the years. My children refer to this as "Mama's Squash Casserole" recipe.

Lois Clark
Cairo, Georgia

BAKED SWEET POTATOES

2-3   large sweet potatoes, peeled and cubed
2   tablespoons olive oil
2   teaspoons brown sugar
1   teaspoon cinnamon
Dash red pepper

Place sweet potatoes in large bowl. Drizzle with olive oil. Combine brown sugar and cinnamon and red pepper. Mix thoroughly with sweet potatoes. Spread sweet potatoes out on baking sheet and bake for 15-20 minutes at 375 degrees.

Norma Crawford Thomas
Bishop, Georgia

Vegetables and Side Dishes

SWEET POTATO CASSEROLE

8	sweet potatoes, peeled, cut into chunks and cooked
½	cup brown sugar
¼	teaspoon salt
½	teaspoon cinnamon
1	egg, beaten
1	tablespoon butter
1	small package miniature marshmallows

Mash sweet potatoes in a bowl. Add brown sugar, salt, cinnamon, egg and butter. Mix well. Grease dish. Place half of mixture in pan. Top with half bag of marshmallows. Add remaining sweet potato mixture on top of marshmallows. Bake at 350 degrees for 30 minutes. Top with remaining marshmallows and bake 10 more minutes.

Sheila Brown
Moultrie, Georgia

SWEET POTATO CASSEROLE

1	(1 pound, 13 ounce) can of whole sweet potatoes, drained
¾	stick butter, softened
2	eggs
Dash of cinnamon	
1	cup evaporated milk
1½	cups sugar

Mix potatoes, butter and eggs well in a small bowl. In another small bowl, mix cinnamon, evaporated milk and sugar; blend in with the potato mixture. Bake at 400 degrees for 15-20 minutes.

Topping:

1	cup crushed corn flakes	½	cup packed brown sugar
½	cup chopped nuts	¾	stick butter

Mix corn flakes, nuts and brown sugar and sprinkle on potatoes. Put pats of butter on topping. Cover with foil and bake an additional 15 minutes. Remove foil and bake an additional 5 minutes.

Margaret Anderson
Meigs, Georgia

SWEET POTATO SOUFFLE

3	cups cooked, mashed sweet potatoes
1	cup sugar
3	eggs
½	cup milk
½	stick butter or margarine
1	tablespoon vanilla extract
½	teaspoon salt

Combine all ingredients, pour into baking dish and top with:

1	cup brown sugar	½	cup self-rising flour
½	stick margarine	1	cup chopped pecans

Mix and blend all ingredients by hand. Then spread mixture over sweet potato mixture. Bake at 350 degrees (about 45 minutes) or until topping is light brown. Recipe can be doubled.

Mary Walker
Tifton, Georgia

MEXICORN CASSEROLE

1	(5-ounce) package yellow rice, cooked as directed
1	can Mexi-corn, do not drain
1	can cream of chicken soup
1	can English peas, drain half of juice
8	ounces sour cream
1	small onion, chopped
1	cup grated Cheddar cheese

Mix all ingredients except cheese. Place in a 2-quart casserole dish and top with cheese. Bake at 350 degrees for 30 – 35 minutes.

Patsy Wester
Meigs, Georgia

Vegetables and Side Dishes

MEXICAN CORN CASSEROLE

1	(5-ounce) package yellow rice
1	can Mexican corn
2	cups sour cream
1	can cream of chicken soup
½	stick butter
1	can water chestnuts
1	cup grated sharp cheese

Cook yellow rice according to package directions. Mix rice, Mexican corn, sour cream, cream of chicken soup, butter and water chestnuts well and pour in baking dish. Top with grated sharp cheese. Bake at 350 degrees for 30 to 40 minutes.

Maurissa Smith
Atlanta, Georgia

VEGETABLE CASSEROLE

(A first edition favorite)

1	package frozen vegetable mixture (carrots, chestnuts and broccoli)
1	can cream of mushroom soup
½	cup sour cream
½	cup mayonnaise
2	cups Monterey Jack cheese
1	onion, chopped

Salt and pepper
| 1 | can dry onion rings |

Cook vegetable mixture according to package directions; drain. Mix all ingredients reserving half of cheese and dry onions rings. Top with remaining cheese and dry onions. Bake 30 minutes. You may wait till the last five minutes to add remaining cheese and dry onions rings.

A family favorite from my sister, Brenda Chandler who lives in Hull, Georgia.

Nancy Coleman
Hartsfield, Georgia

VEGETABLE CASSEROLE SUPREME

(A first edition favorite)

½   cup chopped celery
½   cup chopped onions
¼   cup chopped green pepper
1   can French green beans, drained and rinsed
1   can cream of celery soup
½   cup sour cream
1   cup grated cheese (I use Cracker Barrel sharp)

Stir ingredients together. Pour in a 9x13-inch glass baking dish.

½ stick margarine, melted   ½ cup slivered almonds
½ box Ritz crackers, crushed

Mix cracker crumbs with melted margarine. Sprinkle over casserole. Top with almonds. Bake 45 minutes at 350 degrees. Yield: 10 servings

Judy Mobley
Moultrie, Georgia

CHRISTMAS CASSEROLE

1   large can asparagus, drained
1   large can English peas, drained
1   large jar red diced pimientos, drained

Cheese Sauce

2   cups milk   3   tablespoons flour
3   tablespoons butter   1   cup finely grated extra
                                       sharp cheese

In double boiler melt and stir together the butter and flour. When smooth, slowly add 2 cups of milk, stirring constantly. Stir in cup of grated cheese; heat and stir sauce until cheese is completely melted. In casserole, place one layer of asparagus, then one layer of English peas, followed by one layer of pimientos; cover with half of the cheese sauce. Repeat layers and cover with remaining cheese sauce. Bake at 350 degrees until bubbly.

Brenda Morris
Ocilla, Georgia

Vegetables and Side Dishes

MIXED VEGETABLE CASSEROLE

2   cans mixed vegetables
1   small onion
1   cup grated sharp cheese

Drain the vegetables and pour into mixing bowl. Grate or finely chop the onion. Add to vegetables. Add the 2 cups of grated cheese to the onion/vegetable mixture.

In a separate bowl, mix the following:

¾   cup mayonnaise
2   teaspoons hot sauce
2   teaspoons Worcestershire Sauce
1   teaspoon salt
1   teaspoon pepper

Pour this mixture into the vegetables and stir.

Pour the vegetable mixture into a greased 2 quart casserole dish. Crush one sleeve of Ritz crackers and pour on top of casserole. Dot the crackers with one stick of butter.

This casserole has become a favorite at our house. My best friend asks for it each time she comes to dinner! Since she is not a huge vegetable fan, I always make it for her so she will get some veggies!

Lynn Larsen
DeSoto, Georgia

EASY BROWN RICE

1   cup long grain rice (not instant)
2   cans beef consommé
1   tablespoon butter
Salt to taste

Place rice in baking dish. Add beef consommé. Dot with butter. Salt to taste. Bake at 350 degrees for 1 hour.

Norma Crawford Thomas
Bishop, Georgia

MOM'S BROWN RICE

1   stick margarine, melted
1   chopped onion
1   cup rice
2   cans beef consommé
1   can sliced mushrooms, drained

Sauté onions in butter; add rice and stir until rice looks translucent. Add consommé and mushrooms. Bake at 350 degrees for 55 minutes. This recipe can also be cooked on the stove top.

Maurissa Smith
Atlanta, Georgia

BROWN RICE CASSEROLE

1½   cup uncooked rice
1   stick butter
1   can beef bouillon soup
1   can French onion soup
¼   cup water

Pour rice into a medium sized casserole dish. Melt butter and pour over rice. Pour in beef bouillon soup, French onion soup, and water; stir and cover dish with foil or lid. Bake at 350 degrees for 1½ hours.

This dish is great with roast beef!

Patty Veazey
Tifton, Georgia

SAVORY RICE

½   cup sour cream
¼   cup mayonnaise
1   teaspoon lemon juice
2   tablespoons minced chives or parsley
½   teaspoon salt
¼   cup pimiento strips
3 cups hot, cooked rice

Blend sour cream, mayonnaise, lemon juice, chives, salt and pimiento strips.
Stir into hot cooked rice. Serve immediately. May be packed into 6 half-cup
individual molds. Invert on to plate and garnish with red peppers. Yield: 6
servings

Jane Gibbs
Moultrie, Georgia

SPEEDY FRIED RICE

3   tablespoons oil
3   eggs
1   (16-ounce) package Oriental-style mixed vegetables
½   pound julienned ham
3   cups cooked rice
1   cup chopped scallions
Soy sauce

In large skillet, heat 1 tablespoon oil over medium heat. In bowl, beat 3 large eggs,
add to skillet. Cook until set; place on plate. In same skillet, in 2 tablespoons oil
over medium high heat, stir-fry vegetables until tender and beginning to brown.
Add ham and 3 cups cooked rice. Stir fry 5 minutes or until hot; stir in eggs
until mixed. Serve with soy sauce; sprinkle with chopped scallions.

Mary Walker
Tifton, Georgia

MY FAVORITE SQUASH CASSEROLE

2	pounds squash
¾	cup milk
1	cup chopped onions
12	saltine crackers
2	eggs
1	package ranch dressing mix
½	cup mayonnaise
1	cup cheese
½	cup sour cream
1-2	cups buttered bread crumbs

Mix all ingredients except bread crumbs. Pour into casserole dish sprayed with cooking spray. Top with crumbs. Bake at 350 degrees for 40-45 minutes.

My favorite!

Cathy Thompson
Vienna, Georgia

HAM AND TOMATO PIE

Pastry for 9-inch pie crust

5	tablespoons Dijon mustard
1 ½	cups coarsely chopped ham
5	tablespoons minced parsley
3	tablespoons minced onion
½	cup mayonnaise
2	tomatoes, peeled and thickly sliced
2	tablespoons crushed crackers
1½	cups shredded sharp Cheddar cheese

Salt and pepper to taste

½	teaspoon basil

Bake pie crust, cool, and brush inside with mustard and allow to dry. In a small bowl mix together ham, 1 tablespoon parsley, and 1 tablespoon onion. Spread in shell. Cover with tomato slices and sprinkle with salt and pepper. In a bowl blend cheese, mayonnaise, remaining parsley, onion, crackers and basil. Spread cheese mixture over filling. Bake at 400 degrees for 30-35 minutes.

Great way to use leftover ham. Freezes well, also.

Tammy Thompson Morgan
Charlotte, North Carolina

270

Vegetables and Side Dishes

Everything Else

THE ECONOMY

Valued annually at approximately $745 million, cotton is a leading cash crop in Georgia. This figure includes the value of the lint and seed. With 1.4 million acres, Georgia ranks second behind Texas in cotton acreage. In 2007, cotton production was 1.66 million bales of cotton at an estimated market value of $400.8 million.

The vast cotton industry in the state includes 3,216 farms, 68 gins, 19 merchants, 73 warehouses, 3 cottonseed oil mills and 68 textile mills. These 3,448 businesses account for approximately $2.5 billion in revenue.

Cotton is grown in 91 of Georgia's 159 counties and is more widespread than any other crop. In 2007, the five leading counties in terms of production were: Dooly (103,400 bales), Colquitt (90,200 bales), Worth (89,600), Mitchell (82,200) and Brooks (68,800 bales).

Nationwide, the cotton industry generated $100 billion in revenue for the economy, standing above all crops in the creation of jobs and contributions to our national wealth. The U.S. is the largest exporter of cotton to the world, even though it is third in production to China.

The fiber of a thousand faces and almost as many uses, cotton is noted for its versatility, its appearance, its performance, and – above all—its natural comfort. From all types of apparel, to sheets and towels, tarpaulins and tents, cotton in today's fast-moving world is still nature's wonder fiber, providing thousands of useful products and supporting millions of jobs as it moves year after year from field to fabric.

INDEX

PRALINE SAUCE

¼ cup butter
1   cup brown sugar
⅓ cup whipping cream
1   cup powdered sugar
1   teaspoon vanilla extract

Bring butter, brown sugar and whipping cream to a boil over medium heat, stirring often. Boil for one minute. Remove from heat and add powdered sugar and vanilla. Beat until smooth. If you make ahead, refrigerate at this point. Allow to come to room temperature to serve. Great served over apple pie and sprinkled with toasted pecans.

Virginia Hart
Moultrie, Georgia

JAVA CHOCOLATE SAUCE

1   (12-ounce) package semisweet chocolate chips
½ cup whipping cream
1   tablespoon butter or margarine
¼ cup strong brewed coffee

Heat chocolate chips, cream and butter in a heavy saucepan over low heat until chocolate and butter melt, stirring often. Cook, stirring constantly, 2 to 3 minutes or until smooth. Remove form heat; stir in coffee. Serve warm. Yield: 1 ¼ cups

Good with ice cream or stirred into milk, hot or cold.

Nancy Coleman
Hartsfield, Georgia

COCONUT DIP FOR FRUIT

1   (8 ounce) package cream cheese, softened
1   (8.5 ounce) can cream of coconut (Coco Lopez)
Fruit for dipping

Beat cream cheese with electric mixer until fluffy. Gradually add the cream of coconut, continuing to beat on low speed. Refrigerate until ready to serve.

Suggestion: Serve in compote-style dish and top with just a little flaked coconut. Serve with fresh fruit such as strawberries, sliced apples, pineapple, or your choice. Place compote in middle of tray and surround with assorted fresh fruit.

Gail Thompson
Moultrie, Georgia

PINEAPPLE SAUCE

1   cup brown sugar
1   tablespoon cornstarch
¼   teaspoon salt
1   (8½-ounce) can crushed pineapple, with juice
2   tablespoon lemon juice
1   tablespoon prepared mustard

Mix brown sugar, cornstarch, and salt in a saucepan. Add pineapple juice, lemon juice and prepared mustard. Cook over medium heat stirring constantly until mixture thickens. Cook one minute. Baste on ham during baking. Yield: 1 ¾ cups.

Nancy Coleman
Hartsfield, Georgia

PINEAPPLE BERRY RELISH

1	(20-ounce) can crushed pineapple, drained
2	(16-ounce) can whole cranberry sauce
1	(16-ounce) package frozen strawberries, thawed and drained
½	cup chopped pecans

Mix above ingredients in a bowl and chill. Yield: about 6 cups.

Delicious with turkey or ham.

Charlotte Mathis
Moultrie, Georgia

PLUM SAUCE FOR PORK

2	tablespoons butter
¾	cup chopped onion
1	cup red plum preserves
½	cup brown sugar, packed
⅔	cup water
2	tablespoons lemon juice
⅓	cup chili sauce
¼	cup soy sauce
2	teaspoons prepared mustard
3	drops Tabasco sauce

Melt butter in skillet and sauté onion until tender. Add remaining ingredients;
simmer 15 minutes.

*Sauce is delicious with any cut of pork. Baste meat the last few minutes of
cooking or serve sauce on side.*

Nancy Coleman
Hartsfield, Georgia

HORSERADISH SAUCE

1	cup sour cream
⅓	cup prepared horseradish
1	teaspoon dill weed
1	teaspoon salt
¼	teaspoon pepper

Mix all ingredients. Chill for at least 3 hours. Serve with roast beef or prime rib.

Thomas Coleman
Hartsfield, Georgia

HOT AND SPICY BARBECUE SAUCE
(A first edition favorite)

3	(32-ounce) bottles catsup
Juice from 2 dozen lemons	
1	small bottle hot sauce (Bull's or Louisiana)
1	cup vinegar
3	teaspoons salt
3	teaspoons sugar
½	(1-ounce) box red pepper
3	tablespoons black pepper
1	(15-ounce) bottle Worcestershire sauce

Squeeze juice from lemons. Heat all ingredients in large Dutch oven, but do not boil. Pour into jars and refrigerate to store.

Very hot but great on chopped beef or pork. Can be used on chicken.

Thomas Coleman
Hartsfield, Georgia

THICK AND CHUNKY BARBECUE SAUCE

(A first edition favorite)

¼   cup butter
1   large onion, chopped
1   bell pepper, chopped (optional)
1   cup catsup
¼   cup firmly packed brown sugar
3   tablespoons Worcestershire sauce
1   teaspoon salt
⅛   teaspoon pepper
1 ½ teaspoons chili powder

Melt butter in saucepan. Add onion and bell pepper and sauté until tender; stir in remaining ingredients. Cover and simmer at least 5 minutes. Excellent for chicken, ribs and pork chops. Yield: 1 1/2 cups

When I was in college, friends told me I should bottle this sauce and then retire. Great on chicken and ribs.

Nancy Coleman
Hartsfield, Georgia

PORT WINE MARINADE FOR BEEF

1   fifth bottle white port wine
6   medium bay leaves
2½   tablespoons salt
1   tablespoon minced garlic
4   tablespoons olive oil
4   tablespoons vinegar
2   tablespoons black pepper

Combine all ingredients; bring to a boil. Marinate steaks 10 to 12 hours. Use for basting while cooking; serve with steak also.

Thomas Coleman
Hartsfield, Georgia

FLANK STEAK MARINADE

1   cup oil (olive, preferably)
½   cup soy sauce
1   tablespoon garlic
1   teaspoon dry mustard
2   tablespoons lemon juice

Blend in processor, pour over steak. Marinate 3-4 hours, turning occasionally.

Nancy Coleman
Hartsfield, Georgia

PEAR PICKLES

7 to   10 pounds pears
2½   cups sugar
1½   cups vinegar
2   tablespoons pickling spice
2   tablespoons whole cloves
3   teaspoons cinnamon

Wash, peel, core, and quarter pears. Place in pan of water with Fruit Fresh or lemon juice added to prevent discoloration. Tie spices in cheese cloth. Mix all ingredients except pears. Bring to a boil and add pears. Do not cover. Cook until pears are tender when pierced with a fork. Sterilize jars. Pack pears in jars. Cover with syrup. Seal in hot water bath. Chill before serving.

Pears are plentiful on our farm in the fall. Every old farmstead must have had a pear tree. Other than Pear Pie, this is my favorite way to eat pears.

Nancy Coleman
Hartsfield, Georgia

Everything Else

NO-COOK SWEET AND SPICY PICKLES

1   (46-ounce) jar hamburger dill pickles
½   cup sugar
2   large garlic cloves, thinly sliced
2   tablespoons Tabasco sauce

Drain liquid form jar. Remove pickles from jar; rinse with water and drain.
Layer half each of pickles, sugar, garlic and hot sauce. Press down. Repeat layers.
Put lid on jar and secure. Invert jar and shake until ingredients are combined.
Store in refrigerator.

*Makes a nice homemade gift. Great at fish fries and picnics. Adds a little kick
to your potato salad.*

Nancy Coleman
Hartsfield, Georgia

JUDY'S PEPPER RELISH

24 large red pimentos
12 large onions
4   hot peppers
2   tablespoons celery
2   tablespoons salt
1   quart vinegar
4   cups sugar

Roast pimientos in slow oven. Cool and peel. Coarsely grind pimientos, onions,
and hot peppers. Add remaining ingredients and cook slowly. Stir constantly,
cooking for about 20 minutes after mixture is thoroughly hot. Pour in jars and
seal. This may be doubled easily.

Judy Harris
Cordele, Georgia

RED PEPPER JELLY

5	red bell peppers, seeded, coarsely chopped
10	red jalapeño or Serrano chilies, seeded, coarsely chopped
1 ½	cups cider vinegar
6 ½	cups sugar
2	(3-ounce) boxes fruit pectin

Red food coloring (optional)

Sterilize and prepare canning jars and lids. Place peppers in blender and puree until liquefied. (1 or 2 tablespoons vinegar may help the liquidation process.) Place in 6- or 8-quart saucepan. Add vinegar and stir in sugar while bringing to a full boil. Add pectin and bring to a full boil for 3 minutes. Add food coloring, if used. Remove from heat. Skim foam off top. Ladle immediately into prepared jars (6–8 half-pints). Wipe jar rims and threads. Place 2-piece lids on and screw tight. Process in hot bath for ten minutes.

Note: For Green Pepper Jelly, substitute green bell peppers and green jalapeños. If you would like some texture to the jelly, finely chop one of the bell peppers instead of pureeing and add to mixture.

My husband's cousin, Jerry Griner, makes this for us every summer when peppers are plentiful. It's especially good with Rosalyn Carter's Cheese Ring and other appetizers.

Nancy Coleman
Hartsfield, Georgia

Everything Else

KUMQUAT MARMALADE

3	cups seeded and chopped kumquats
1	cup water
6 ½	cups sugar
1	box powdered fruit pectin such as Sure Jell

Prepare kumquats by cutting fruit in half to remove seeds; chop coarsely or slice thinly (can be put through food chopper). Combine chopped kumquats, water and fruit pectin. Add sugar and bring to boil that cannot be stirred down. Continue to boil for one minute. Pour into sterile jars. Wipe off rims. Seal with two piece lids and process in hot water bath according to manufacturer's directions. It may take up to a week to gel. Even if it doesn't get as thick as you'd like, it's still very good on hot toast or biscuits.

My parents have two huge kumquat trees at their home in Cairo. They have babied them over the years to protect them from the occasional South Georgia hard freeze. Marmalade allows us to enjoy the kumquats year round.

Nancy Coleman
Hartsfield, Georgia

If you don't have cheesecloth to make a spice bag while making pickles, use a new, inexpensive knee high hose. Rinse before using. Stretch it over the top of a short class to making filling it easier. Tie the top with a knot, cut of excess. When finished with the pickling process, discard the spice bag.

MAYHAW JELLY

Juice:

3   pounds mayhaw berries
4   cups water

Wash berries. Place berries in a large pot and crush with potato masher or something similar. Add water to berries. Bring to boil, cover and simmer for 10 minutes, stirring occasionally. Strain juice, using cheesecloth, into another pot. When juice stops dripping, squeeze cloth to get remaining juice. Discard berries.

Jelly:

4   cups mayhaw juice
1   box fruit pectin
5 ½ cups sugar

Place mayhaw juice in a 6-8 quart saucepan. Stir in fruit pectin. Bring to a full boil over high heat, stirring occasionally. Stir in sugar all at once and continue stirring until you have a full, rolling boil. Continue to boil for 1 minute, stirring constantly. Remove from heat; skim off foam immediately and ladle into hot, sterile jars. Wipe off rims. Seal with two piece lids and process in hot water bath according to manufacturer's directions.

Nancy Coleman
Hartsfield, Georgia

The King of all Sandwiches
Elvis Presley's Favorite

GRILLED PEANUT BUTTER AND BANANA SANDWICH

6-8   tablespoons smooth or crunchy peanut butter
8   slices whole grain bread
2   large ripe bananas, sliced lengthwise
2   tablespoons honey (may be omitted)

Spread peanut butter on each slice of bread. Place banana pieces on top of the peanut butter on four of the slices and drizzle with honey. Press the remaining slices of bread on top to make four sandwiches. Place a large, nonstick skillet over medium high heat. Coat the bread with cooking spray just before browning each side. Sauté or grill sandwiches until golden brown. Slice the sandwiches and serve warm. Yield: 4 sandwiches

Brenda Morris
Ocilla, Georgia

Index

THE PEOPLE

People in the cotton industry are as varied as the uses of cotton. While those employed in the industry range from farmers to textile mill workers, those involved in cotton at the "roots" are the producers. These are the people with rich Georgia soil under their fingernails and, if someone were to look closely enough, they would probably find cottonseed oil running through their veins. As farmers are prone to say about farming, "It's in my blood."

Cotton farms range in size from 30-40 acres to thousands of acres. Some cotton farmers have been growing cotton for generations while others are relative newcomers. Whether picking or ginning, cotton harvest means long hours, late suppers and missed ballgames. Nothing makes a cotton farmer happier than the sight of another module of cotton emerging from the module builder as the cotton pickers continue to roll across the field.

While being around farm equipment is not an acceptable practice for farm children, they too are fascinated at the sights and sounds of cotton harvesting. This early interest may explain why farmers say "it's in my blood."

Women in the cotton industry are largely behind-the-scenes workers, but not so for the members of Georgia Cotton Women, Inc. These women devote hours to promoting cotton and educating the next generation of cotton consumers.

For many Georgians, cotton is a family business. That keeps both the industry and the families strong.

Appetizers

Beverages

Breads

Cakes and Frostings

Candies

Cookies

Desserts and Pies

Entrees

Beef

To order additional copies, make checks payable to:
Father & Son Publishing, Inc. and mail to:
4909 North Monroe Street ◆ Tallahassee, Florida 32303

Please send me _____ copies of *Cooking in High Cotton* @ $19.95 plus $3.00 each for
postage and handling. Florida and Georgia residents add 7% sales tax.
Enclosed is my check or money order for $_____

Name _____

Address_____ Phone _____

City_____ State _____ Zip _____

MasterCard/Visa Card # _____CV Code _____

Exp. date _____ Signature _____

— —

To order additional copies, make checks payable to:
Father & Son Publishing, Inc. and mail to:
4909 North Monroe Street ◆ Tallahassee, Florida 32303

Please send me _____ copies of *Cooking in High Cotton* @ $19.95 plus $3.00 each for
postage and handling. Florida and Georgia residents add 7% sales tax.
Enclosed is my check or money order for $_____

Name _____

Address_____ Phone _____

City_____ State _____ Zip _____

MasterCard/Visa Card # _____CV Code _____

Exp. date _____ Signature _____

— —

To order additional copies, make checks payable to:
Father & Son Publishing, Inc. and mail to:
4909 North Monroe Street ◆ Tallahassee, Florida 32303

Please send me _____ copies of *Cooking in High Cotton* @ $19.95 plus $3.00 each for
postage and handling. Florida and Georgia residents add 7% sales tax.
Enclosed is my check or money order for $_____

Name _____

Address_____ Phone _____

City_____ State _____ Zip _____

MasterCard/Visa Card # _____CV Code _____

Exp. date _____ Signature _____

— —